HOUGHTON MIFFLIN HARCOURT

Comprehensive Language and Literacy Guide

Consultant
Irene C. Fountas

Grade 1

Printed in the U.S.A.

ISBN 13: 978-0-547-24108-1
ISBN 10: 0-547-24108-9

5 6 7 8 9 10 0877 18 17 16 15 14 13 12   4500350097

HOUGHTON MIFFLIN HARCOURT
School Publishers

Comprehensive Language and Literacy Guide

A Readers' Workshop Approach

Introduction: What Are Effective Instructional Practices in Literacy? 1

• Whole-Group Teaching 2
• Small-Group Teaching 4
• Independent Literacy Work 6

Planning for Comprehensive Language and Literacy Instruction 8

Whole-Group Lessons 39

• Interactive Read-Aloud/Shared Reading
• Reading Minilessons

Teaching Genre 101

Appendix 112

• Leveled Readers Database 112
• Literature Discussion: Suggested Trade Book Titles 124
• Professional Bibliography 129

Introduction

What Are Effective Instructional Practices in Literacy?

Your goal in literacy teaching is to bring each child from where he is to as far as you can take him in a school year, with the clear goal of helping each student develop the competencies of proficiency at the level. Proficient readers and writers not only think deeply and critically about texts but also develop a love of reading. The roots of lifelong literacy begin with a rich foundation in the elementary school.

The Comprehensive Language and Literacy Guide provides a structure for organizing your literacy teaching, linking understandings across the language and literacy framework, and building a strong foundation of reading strategies and skills. On the pages that follow, you will find an overview of how to use this guide along with your *Journeys* materials in three different instructional contexts: Whole-Group Teaching, Small-Group Teaching, and Independent Literacy Work.

WHOLE GROUP
Interactive Read-Aloud/Shared Reading
(heterogeneous)

WHOLE GROUP
Reading Minilesson
(heterogeneous)

SMALL GROUP
Guided Reading
(temporary homogeneous)

SMALL GROUP
Literature Discussion
(heterogeneous)

INDEPENDENT
Independent Reading,
Independent Literacy Work

Whole-Group Teaching

👤 TEACHER'S ROLE

- Engage children in thinking deeply about texts.
- Provide a learning environment in which children feel comfortable sharing their thinking with each other.
- Prepare explicit lessons that are tailored to children's needs.
- Provide a model of phrased, fluent reading in interactive read-aloud.
- Prompt children with comments and questions at planned stopping points to promote active thinking in interactive read-aloud/shared reading.
- Provide explicit teaching of critical literacy concepts in reading minilessons.
- Expose children to a wide variety of genres, authors, and topics.
- Monitor children's understanding to plan for future lessons.

👥 CHILD'S ROLE

- Listen actively.
- Share ideas and opinions with others.
- Make connections to other readings and to own experiences.
- Ask genuine questions and build on the ideas of others.
- Demonstrate understanding of critical literacy concepts.

Whole-group lessons lay the foundation for the day's instruction and give children the tools they will need to apply what they have learned in other contexts, including small-group instruction and independent literacy work.

PLANNING FOR COMPREHENSIVE LANGUAGE & LITERACY INSTRUCTION
For each lesson, or week of instruction, select from the menu of items shown on the Suggested Weekly Focus page, or use all of them.

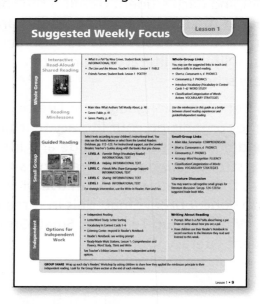

◀ Plan whole-group teaching using the menu of options provided.

WHOLE-GROUP LESSONS The Whole-Group Lessons are related lesson sequences you may want to use across a week. At the core of each lesson is a *Journeys* literature selection, chosen to highlight a certain aspect of reading that is important for children to learn and apply in various contexts.

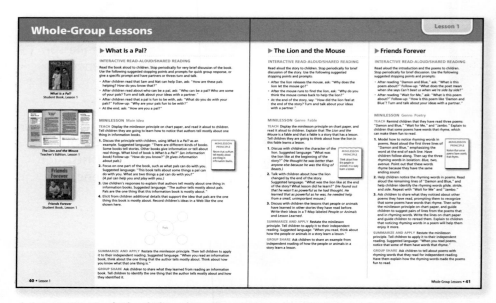

▲ Interactive Read-Aloud/Shared Reading and Reading Minilessons build and expand children's understandings, using a *Journeys* literature selection.

Parts of Whole-Group Lessons

1 **Interactive Read-Aloud/Shared Reading** sets the stage for the day's focus and provides a common foundation of experience for children at various levels of reading proficiency (Fountas and Pinnell, 2006). In Interactive Read-Aloud/Shared Reading, you read aloud to children and encourage discussion of the reading through questions and prompts at planned stopping points in the text. Reading aloud to children in this context will help them appreciate literature, and they benefit from your modeling of how to think about ideas in the text as well as from the thinking of their peers. In addition, Interactive Read-Aloud/Shared Reading

- serves as a model of fluent, expressive, phrased reading.
- provides a context for getting children to think actively about what they read.
- allows children to hear a variety of perspectives and interpretations.
- is the common text used as an example in the Reading Minilesson.

2 The **Reading Minilesson** is the second part of your lesson. The minilesson is focused instruction about a specific topic or skill, called the Minilesson Principle (Fountas and Pinnell, 2001). Using this principle, you help children think like effective, independent readers. The literature selection from Interactive Read-Aloud/Shared Reading context is used as the example to demonstrate the principle.

TEACHING GENRE Genre instruction is a powerful tool for helping children develop the competencies of effective readers and writers. The questions and teaching points in this section can be used over and over across the year as children encounter different genres and increasingly difficult texts within a particular genre.

▲ Integrate meaningful genre instruction into your whole-group teaching. Select from the teaching points, questions, and materials provided.

Small-Group Teaching

Small-group lessons are the individualized sessions in which you help children develop as readers based on their needs, challenges, and sometimes their preferences.

GUIDED READING In guided reading lessons, you use *Journeys* Leveled Readers to work with small groups of children who will benefit from teaching at a particular instructional level. You select the text and guide the readers by supporting their ability to use a variety of reading strategies (Fountas and Pinnell, 1996, 2001). Guided reading groups are flexible and should change as a result of your observations of your students' growth.

In this guide, whole-group lessons provide the foundation for small-group instruction. Skills introduced in whole group can be developed and expanded according to children's needs in a smaller group with the appropriate level text. On the Suggested Weekly Focus pages, Leveled Readers that connect to the whole-group experience are suggested, though you may need to select from the complete Leveled Readers Database (pp. 112–123) to match your children's instructional levels.

PLANNING AND RESOURCES Using the small-group resources in this guide, along with the Leveled Readers and the Leveled Readers Teacher's Guides, you can plan for and teach lessons that will develop the competencies of your particular students.

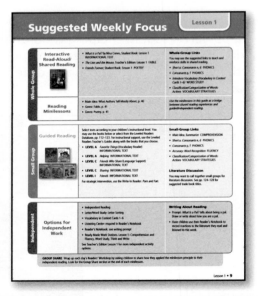

◀ Plan small-group teaching by considering the options on the Suggested Weekly Focus or in the complete Leveled Readers Database.

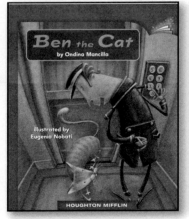
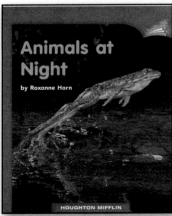

◀ JOURNEYS Leveled Readers Select Leveled Readers according to the instructional levels of your students.

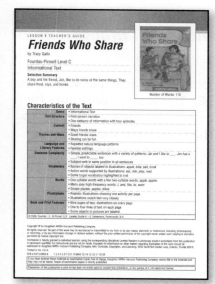

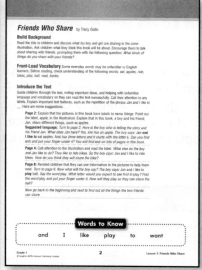

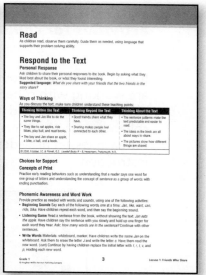

▲ **JOURNEYS Leveled Readers Teacher's Guides**
Support children as they read Leveled Readers at their instructional
level. Use lessons in the Leveled Readers Teacher's Guides to promote
the following:

- Thinking Within the Text
- Thinking Beyond the Text
- Thinking About the Text
- Writing About Reading
- English Language Development
- Phrased, Fluent Reading

LITERATURE DISCUSSION Literature discussion brings together a small group of
children of varying abilities but who may have a common interest—a topic, a genre, or
author. Children have selected the same book to read and have prepared to discuss it. In
this collaborative group, you facilitate discussion of the book and encourage children to
share their thinking and to build upon each other's ideas as they gain a deeper
understanding of the text (Fountas and Pinnell, 2001).

The members of literature discussion groups will change as children select different titles
or topics. One advantage of Literature Discussion is that all readers can benefit from
each other's thinking, regardless of their instructional level.

It is important to guide children in selecting books. Introducing a range of books
through book talks is one way of sharing several options for reading. Encourage
children to sample a book, or read a short segment, to determine whether it is too easy
or too difficult before they make a final selection. If a text choice is hard for the student
to read, someone can read the text to him or her at school or at home.

A wealth of trade books can be used for engaging literature discussions. The Suggested
Trade Book Titles on pp. 124–128 are appropriate for Grade 1 students, and a wide
variety of genres, authors, and topics are represented. Select books from this list and
make them available for children, or use books in your library.

Independent Literacy Work

👤 TEACHER'S ROLE

- Establish classroom routines for independent work time.
- Set expectations for what children should accomplish.
- Confer with individual children to discuss books or sample oral reading.

👥 CHILD'S ROLE

- Follow established classroom routines.
- Engage thoughtfully in reading and writing tasks.
- Take responsibility for assignments, and demonstrate progress.

Independent literacy work includes meaningful and productive activities for children to do while you work with small groups.

It is important that your students engage in meaningful, productive activities when you are working with other children (Fountas and Pinnell, 1996). This is an opportunity for your students to build mileage as readers, to develop good independent work skills, to collaborate with others, and to work at their own pace. The Suggested Weekly Focus for each lesson provides options for independent work that expand on the week's instruction.

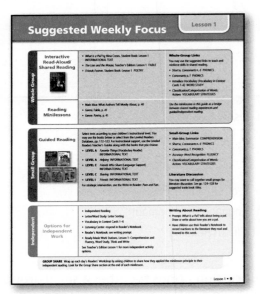

◀ Select from the options for independent work that align with instructional goals.

INDEPENDENT READING The best way to develop reading skills is to read more. Independent reading is a time for children to explore their interests, select books that are "just right" for them, and read continuous text for an established period of time. Support your students as they make book choices because too-hard books will only frustrate them. Teach them how to choose books that they can read with understanding and that don't present too many challenges. Having a large, accessible collection of books—whether in your classroom or in the library—is the best way to support readers.

READER'S NOTEBOOK A Reader's Notebook is a place for children to respond to their reading and to provide evidence of their understanding. The options for what children may write are endless—drawings, letters to you, lists, stories, and sentences. You may ask them to write about something specific or leave it open for the child to choose. A suggested prompt that links to the week's reading is provided on each Suggested Weekly Focus page.

LISTENING CENTER Using a Listening Center will improve children's listening comprehension and expand their vocabulary. It is also an effective way to have children listen to models of fluent reading. Children may respond to the story or book in their Reader's Notebook.

LETTER/WORD STUDY Expose children to a wide variety of meaningful word study activities. Letter sorting, word sorting, identifying rhyming words, compound words, and alphabetical order are just some examples of topics that can be developed into independent literacy activities. The Vocabulary in Context Cards for a given lesson contain high-frequency words used in the week's literature. On the back of each card, a student-friendly explanation of the word and activities are provided to help children think about how the word can be used in various contexts.

▲ Vocabulary in Context Cards

READY-MADE WORK STATIONS The *Journeys* Ready-Made Work Stations link to the week's literature and skills in three strands of literacy instruction: comprehension and fluency, word study, and writing. Three different activities are provided on each card, providing children with multiple opportunities to practice the skill.

▲ Ready-Made Work Stations

Planning for Comprehensive Language and Literacy Instruction

Effective teaching begins with careful observation of your students' literacy behaviors, systematic initial and ongoing assessment, and thoughtful planning to meet the literacy needs of your students. In this guide, you will find a consistent structure and a rich collection of resources with a menu of items and lessons to guide your teaching. You will need to tailor your teaching decisions within the lessons to fit the strengths and needs of your particular students.

On the pages that follow, you will find a Suggested Weekly Focus for each lesson. Options are included for each part of the Readers' Workshop.

- **Whole-Group Teaching:** Interactive Read-Aloud/Shared Reading, Reading Minilessons, Suggested Links for Teaching and Reinforcing Skills
- **Small-Group Teaching:** Guided Reading and Literature Discussion, Suggested Links for Teaching and Reinforcing Skills
- **Independent Work:** Independent Reading, Writing About Reading, Word Study, Ready-Made Work Stations, Vocabulary in Context Cards

Suggested Weekly Focus

Lesson 1	9	Lesson 16	24
Lesson 2	10	Lesson 17	25
Lesson 3	11	Lesson 18	26
Lesson 4	12	Lesson 19	27
Lesson 5	13	Lesson 20	28
Lesson 6	14	Lesson 21	29
Lesson 7	15	Lesson 22	30
Lesson 8	16	Lesson 23	31
Lesson 9	17	Lesson 24	32
Lesson 10	18	Lesson 25	33
Lesson 11	19	Lesson 26	34
Lesson 12	20	Lesson 27	35
Lesson 13	21	Lesson 28	36
Lesson 14	22	Lesson 29	37
Lesson 15	23	Lesson 30	38

Suggested Weekly Focus

Whole Group

Interactive Read-Aloud/ Shared Reading

- *What Is a Pal?* by Nina Crews, Student Book: Lesson 1 INFORMATIONAL TEXT
- *The Lion and the Mouse,* Teacher's Edition: Lesson 1 FABLE
- *Friends Forever,* Student Book: Lesson 1 POETRY

Whole-Group Links

You may use the suggested links to teach and reinforce skills in shared reading.

- *Short* a; *Consonants* n, d PHONICS
- *Consonants* p, f PHONICS
- *Introduce Vocabulary (Vocabulary in Context Cards 1–6)* WORD STUDY
- *Classification/Categorization of Words: Actions* VOCABULARY STRATEGIES

Reading Minilessons

- Main Idea: What Authors Tell Mostly About, p. 40
- Genre: Fable, p. 41
- Genre: Poetry, p. 41

Use the minilessons in this guide as a bridge between shared reading experiences and guided/independent reading.

Small Group

Guided Reading

Select texts according to your children's instructional level. You may use the books below or select from the Leveled Readers Database, pp. 112–123. For instructional support, use the Leveled Readers Teacher's Guides along with the books that you choose.

- **LEVEL A** *Helping* INFORMATIONAL TEXT
- **LEVEL B** *Favorite Things* (Vocabulary Reader) INFORMATIONAL TEXT
- **LEVEL C** *Friends Who Share* (Language Support) INFORMATIONAL TEXT
- **LEVEL C** *Sharing* INFORMATIONAL TEXT
- **LEVEL I** *Friends* INFORMATIONAL TEXT

For strategic intervention, use the Write-In Reader: *Pam and Fan.*

Small-Group Links

- *Main Idea; Summarize* COMPREHENSION
- *Short* a; *Consonants* n, d PHONICS
- *Consonants* p, f PHONICS
- *Accuracy: Word Recognition* FLUENCY
- *Classification/Categorization of Words: Actions* VOCABULARY STRATEGIES

Literature Discussion

You may want to call together small groups for literature discussion. See pp. 124–128 for suggested trade book titles.

Independent

Options for Independent Work

- Independent Reading
- Letter/Word Study: Letter Sorting
- Vocabulary in Context Cards 1–6
- Listening Center: respond in Reader's Notebook
- Reader's Notebook: see writing prompt
- Ready-Made Work Stations, Lesson 1: Comprehension and Fluency, Word Study, Think and Write

See Teacher's Edition Lesson 1 for more independent activity options.

Writing About Reading

- Prompt: *What Is a Pal?* tells about being a pal. Draw or write about how you are a pal.
- Have children use their Reader's Notebook to record reactions to the literature they read and listened to this week.

GROUP SHARE Wrap up each day's Readers' Workshop by asking children to share how they applied the minilesson principle to their independent reading. Look for the Group Share section at the end of each minilesson.

Suggested Weekly Focus

Whole Group

Interactive Read-Aloud/ Shared Reading

- *The Storm* by Raúl Colón, Student Book: Lesson 2 REALISTIC FICTION
- *Susie and the Bandits,* Teacher's Edition: Lesson 2 FANTASY
- *Storms!,* Student Book: Lesson 2 INFORMATIONAL TEXT

Whole-Group Links

You may use the suggested links to teach and reinforce skills in shared reading.

- *Short* i; *Consonants* r, h, /z/s PHONICS
- *Consonants* b, g PHONICS
- *Introduce Vocabulary (Vocabulary in Context Cards 7–12)* WORD STUDY
- *Context Clues* VOCABULARY STRATEGIES

Reading Minilessons

- Understanding Characters: How People and Animals Feel, p. 42
- Understanding Characters: What Characters Do, p. 43
- Genre: Informational Text, p. 43

Use the minilessons in this guide as a bridge between shared reading experiences and guided/ independent reading.

Small Group

Guided Reading

Select texts according to your children's instructional level. You may use the books below or select from the Leveled Readers Database, pp. 112–123. For instructional support, use the Leveled Readers Teacher's Guides along with the books that you choose.

- **LEVEL A** *Granny* REALISTIC FICTION
- **LEVEL B** *Grandpa* (Vocabulary Reader) INFORMATIONAL TEXT
- **LEVEL C** *Grandpa and Me* REALISTIC FICTION
- **LEVEL C** *When Grandpa Was a Boy* (Language Support) REALISTIC FICTION
- **LEVEL J** *A Mexican Festival* REALISTIC FICTION

For strategic intervention, use the Write-In Reader: *Pip Can Help.*

Small-Group Links

- *Understanding Characters; Infer/Predict* COMPREHENSION
- *Short* i; *Consonants* r, h, /z/s PHONICS
- *Consonants* b, g PHONICS
- *Accuracy: Words Connected in Text* FLUENCY
- *Context Clues* VOCABULARY STRATEGIES

Literature Discussion

You may want to call together small groups for literature discussion. See pp. 124–128 for suggested trade book titles.

Independent

Options for Independent Work

- Independent Reading
- Letter/Word Study: Letter Sorting
- Vocabulary in Context Cards 7–12
- Listening Center: respond in Reader's Notebook
- Reader's Notebook: see writing prompt
- Ready-Made Work Stations, Lesson 2: Comprehension and Fluency, Word Study, Think and Write

See Teacher's Edition Lesson 2 for more independent activity options.

Writing About Reading

- Prompt: *Storms!* tells about different kinds of storms. Draw or write about a storm you have seen. Show or write about how you felt during the storm.
- Have children use their Reader's Notebook to record reactions to the literature they read and listened to this week.

GROUP SHARE Wrap up each day's Readers' Workshop by asking children to share how they applied the minilesson principle to their independent reading. Look for the Group Share section at the end of each minilesson.

Suggested Weekly Focus

Whole Group

Interactive Read-Aloud/ Shared Reading

- *Curious George at School* by Margret and H.A. Rey, Student Book: Lesson 3 FANTASY
- *Stone Stew*, Teacher's Edition: Lesson 3 FOLKTALE
- *School Long Ago*, Student Book: Lesson 3 INFORMATIONAL TEXT

Whole-Group Links

You may use the suggested links to teach and reinforce skills in shared reading.

- *Short* o; *Consonants* l, x PHONICS
- *Inflection* -s PHONICS
- *Introduce Vocabulary (Vocabulary in Context Cards 13–18)* WORD STUDY
- *Multiple-Meaning Words* VOCABULARY STRATEGIES

Reading Minilessons

- Sequence of Events: What Happens First, Next, and Last, p. 44
- Sequence of Events: What Happens First, Next, and Last, p. 45
- Genre: Informational Text, p. 45

Use the minilessons in this guide as a bridge between shared reading experiences and guided/ independent reading.

Small Group

Guided Reading

Select texts according to your children's instructional level. You may use the books below or select from the Leveled Readers Database, pp. 112–123. For instructional support, use the Leveled Readers Teacher's Guides along with the books that you choose.

- **LEVEL B** *Curious About School* (Vocabulary Reader) INFORMATIONAL TEXT
- **LEVEL B** *Curious George Finds Out About School* FANTASY
- **LEVEL C** *Curious George Visits School* (Language Support) FANTASY
- **LEVEL C** *Curious George's Day at School* FANTASY
- **LEVEL I** *Curious George at the Library* FANTASY

For strategic intervention, use the Write-In Reader: *Bad Cat*.

Small-Group Links

- *Sequence of Events; Monitor/Clarify* COMPREHENSION
- *Short* o; *Consonants* l, x PHONICS
- *Inflection* -s PHONICS
- *Phrasing: Punctuation* FLUENCY
- *Multiple-Meaning Words* VOCABULARY STRATEGIES

Literature Discussion

You may want to call together small groups for literature discussion. See pp. 124–128 for suggested trade book titles.

Independent

Options for Independent Work

- Independent Reading
- Letter/Word Study: Letter Sorting
- Vocabulary in Context Cards 13–18
- Listening Center: respond in Reader's Notebook
- Reader's Notebook: see writing prompt
- Ready-Made Work Stations, Lesson 3: Comprehension and Fluency, Word Study, Think and Write

See Teacher's Edition Lesson 3 for more independent activity options.

Writing About Reading

- Prompt: *Curious George at School* tells about how children in a class help Curious George solve his problem. Draw or write about a problem in school and how you helped solve it.
- Have children use their Reader's Notebook to record reactions to the literature they read and listened to this week.

GROUP SHARE Wrap up each day's Readers' Workshop by asking children to share how they applied the minilesson principle to their independent reading. Look for the Group Share section at the end of each minilesson.

Whole Group

Interactive Read-Aloud/ Shared Reading

- *Lucia's Neighborhood* by George Ancona, Student Book: Lesson 4 INFORMATIONAL TEXT
- *Painting Word Pictures,* Teacher's Edition: Lesson 4 POETRY
- *City Mouse and Country Mouse* retold by Debbie O'Brien, Student Book: Lesson 4 FABLE

Whole-Group Links

You may use the suggested links to teach and reinforce skills in shared reading.

- *Short* e; *Consonants* y, w PHONICS
- *Consonants* k, v, j PHONICS
- *Introduce Vocabulary (Vocabulary in Context Cards 19–24)* WORD STUDY
- *Alphabetical Order* VOCABULARY STRATEGIES

Reading Minilessons

- Text and Graphic Features: Looking at the Pictures to Understand the Words, p. 46
- Genre: Poetry, p. 47
- Genre: Fable, p. 47

Use the minilessons in this guide as a bridge between shared reading experiences and guided/ independent reading.

Small Group

Guided Reading

Select texts according to your children's instructional level. You may use the books below or select from the Leveled Readers Database, pp. 112–123. For instructional support, use the Leveled Readers Teacher's Guides along with the books that you choose.

- **LEVEL A** *At the Park* INFORMATIONAL TEXT
- **LEVEL C** *Firehouse* (Vocabulary Reader) INFORMATIONAL TEXT
- **LEVEL C** *Our Town* INFORMATIONAL TEXT
- **LEVEL C** *The Places in Our Town* (Language Support) INFORMATIONAL TEXT
- **LEVEL I** *Neighbors* INFORMATIONAL TEXT

For strategic intervention, use the Write-In Reader: *Dex.*

Small-Group Links

- *Text and Graphic Features; Question* COMPREHENSION
- *Short* e; *Consonants* y, w PHONICS
- *Consonants* k, v, j PHONICS
- *Intonation* FLUENCY
- *Alphabetical Order* VOCABULARY STRATEGIES

Literature Discussion

You may want to call together small groups for literature discussion. See pp. 124–128 for suggested trade book titles.

Independent

Options for Independent Work

- Independent Reading
- Letter/Word Study: Letter Sorting
- Vocabulary in Context Cards 19–24
- Listening Center: respond in Reader's Notebook
- Reader's Notebook: see writing prompt
- Ready-Made Work Stations, Lesson 4: Comprehension and Fluency, Word Study, Think and Write

See Teacher's Edition Lesson 4 for more independent activity options.

Writing About Reading

- Prompt: Look at the bakery page in *Lucia's Neighborhood.* Draw and label a picture of a place you visit in your neighborhood.
- Have children use their Reader's Notebook to record reactions to the literature they read and listened to this week.

GROUP SHARE Wrap up each day's Readers' Workshop by asking children to share how they applied the minilesson principle to their independent reading. Look for the Group Share section at the end of each minilesson.

Whole Group

Interactive Read-Aloud/ Shared Reading

- *Gus Takes the Train* by Russel Benfanti, Student Book: Lesson 5 FANTASY
- *Training Around the Town,* Teacher's Edition: Lesson 5 INFORMATIONAL TEXT
- *City Zoo,* Student Book: Lesson 5 INFORMATIONAL TEXT

Whole-Group Links

You may use the suggested links to teach and reinforce skills in shared reading.

- *Short* u PHONICS
- *Consonants* qu, z PHONICS
- *Introduce Vocabulary (Vocabulary in Context Cards 25–30)* WORD STUDY
- *Antonyms* VOCABULARY STRATEGIES

Reading Minilessons

- Story Structure: How a Story Begins and Ends, p. 48
- Genre: Informational Text, p. 49
- Genre: Informational Text, p. 49

Use the minilessons in this guide as a bridge between shared reading experiences and guided/ independent reading.

Small Group

Guided Reading

Select texts according to your children's instructional level. You may use the books below or select from the Leveled Readers Database, pp. 112–123. For instructional support, use the Leveled Readers Teacher's Guides along with the books that you choose.

- **LEVEL A** *Sledding* FANTASY
- **LEVEL C** *Trains* (Vocabulary Reader) INFORMATIONAL TEXT
- **LEVEL D** *Ben the Cat* FANTASY
- **LEVEL D** *A Cat Named Ben* (Language Support) FANTASY
- **LEVEL J** *A Job for Jojo* FANTASY

For strategic intervention, use the Write-In Reader: *Sal.*

Small-Group Links

- *Story Structure; Analyze/Evaluate* COMPREHENSION
- *Short* u PHONICS
- *Consonants* qu, z PHONICS
- *Accuracy: Self-Correct* FLUENCY
- *Antonyms* VOCABULARY STRATEGIES

Literature Discussion

You may want to call together small groups for literature discussion. See pp. 124–128 for suggested trade book titles.

Independent

Options for Independent Work

- Independent Reading
- Letter/Word Study: Letter Sorting
- Vocabulary in Context Cards 25–30
- Listening Center: respond in Reader's Notebook
- Reader's Notebook: see writing prompt
- Ready-Made Work Stations, Lesson 5: Comprehension and Fluency, Word Study, Think and Write

See Teacher's Edition Lesson 5 for more independent activity options.

Writing About Reading

- Prompt: In *Gus Takes the Train*, Gus takes a train trip to the zoo. Draw or write about a trip you have taken. Show or tell about where you went and how you got there.
- Have children use their Reader's Notebook to record reactions to the literature they read and listened to this week.

GROUP SHARE Wrap up each day's Readers' Workshop by asking children to share how they applied the minilesson principle to their independent reading. Look for the Group Share section at the end of each minilesson.

Whole Group

Interactive Read-Aloud/ Shared Reading

- *Jack and the Wolf* by Chris Sheban, Student Book: Lesson 6 FABLE
- *Night of the Wolf*, Teacher's Edition: Lesson 6 REALISTIC FICTION
- *The Three Little Pigs*, Student Book: Lesson 6 FAIRY TALE

Whole-Group Links

You may use the suggested links to teach and reinforce skills in shared reading.

- *Review Short* a PHONICS
- *Double Final Consonants and* ck PHONICS
- *Introduce Vocabulary (Vocabulary in Context Cards 31–36)* WORD STUDY
- *Classification/Categorization of Words: Actions* VOCABULARY STRATEGIES

Reading Minilessons

- Understanding Characters: How Characters Change, p. 50
- Understanding Characters: How Characters Are Like Real People, p. 51
- Genre: Fairy Tale, p. 51

Use the minilessons in this guide as a bridge between shared reading experiences and guided/ independent reading.

Small Group

Guided Reading

Select texts according to your children's instructional level. You may use the books below or select from the Leveled Readers Database, pp. 112–123. For instructional support, use the Leveled Readers Teacher's Guides along with the books that you choose.

- **LEVEL B**   *The Pigs* FABLE
- **LEVEL D**   *Go Turtle! Go Hare!* (Language Support) FABLE
- **LEVEL D**   *Reading* (Vocabulary Reader) INFORMATIONAL TEXT
- **LEVEL D**   *Turtle and Hare* FABLE
- **LEVEL I**   *Fox and Crow* FABLE

For strategic intervention, use the Write-In Reader: *Run, Run, Run!*

Small-Group Links

- *Understanding Characters; Summarize* COMPREHENSION
- *Review Short* a PHONICS
- *Double Final Consonants and* ck PHONICS
- *Expression* FLUENCY
- *Classification/Categorization of Words: Actions* VOCABULARY STRATEGIES

Literature Discussion

You may want to call together small groups for literature discussion. See pp. 124–128 for suggested trade book titles.

Independent

Options for Independent Work

- Independent Reading
- Letter/Word Study: Letter Sorting
- Vocabulary in Context Cards 31–36
- Listening Center: respond in Reader's Notebook
- Reader's Notebook: see writing prompt
- Ready-Made Work Stations, Lesson 6: Comprehension and Fluency, Word Study, Think and Write

See Teacher's Edition Lesson 6 for more independent activity options.

Writing About Reading

- Prompt: *Jack and the Wolf* is a story that has a lesson. Draw or write about the lesson Jack learned. Tell why it is important.
- Have children use their Reader's Notebook to record reactions to the literature they read and listened to this week.

GROUP SHARE Wrap up each day's Readers' Workshop by asking children to share how they applied the minilesson principle to their independent reading. Look for the Group Share section at the end of each minilesson.

Whole Group

Interactive Read-Aloud/ Shared Reading

- *How Animals Communicate* by William Muñoz, Student Book: Lesson 7 INFORMATIONAL TEXT
- *Prairie Dogs*, Teacher's Edition: Lesson 7 INFORMATIONAL TEXT
- *Insect Messages*, Student Book: Lesson 7 INFORMATIONAL TEXT

Whole-Group Links

You may use the suggested links to teach and reinforce skills in shared reading.

- *Review Short* i PHONICS
- *Clusters with* r PHONICS
- *Introduce Vocabulary (Vocabulary in Context Cards 37–42)* WORD STUDY
- *Using a Glossary* VOCABULARY STRATEGIES

Reading Minilessons

- Details: How Things Look, Feel, Sound, and Smell, p. 52
- Details: Describing Words, p. 53
- Genre: Informational Text, p. 53

Use the minilessons in this guide as a bridge between shared reading experiences and guided/ independent reading.

Small Group

Guided Reading

Select texts according to your children's instructional level. You may use the books below or select from the Leveled Readers Database, pp. 112–123. For instructional support, use the Leveled Readers Teacher's Guides along with the books that you choose.

- **LEVEL B** *Dogs* INFORMATIONAL TEXT
- **LEVEL C** *Animal Talk* (Vocabulary Reader) INFORMATIONAL TEXT
- **LEVEL D** *Animals at Night* INFORMATIONAL TEXT
- **LEVEL D** *Busy Animals at Night* (Language Support) INFORMATIONAL TEXT
- **LEVEL J** *Dog Talk* INFORMATIONAL TEXT

For strategic intervention, use the Write-In Reader: *Tell Cat!*

Small-Group Links

- *Details; Infer/Predict* COMPREHENSION
- *Review Short* i PHONICS
- *Clusters with* r PHONICS
- *Rate* FLUENCY
- *Using a Glossary* VOCABULARY STRATEGIES

Literature Discussion

You may want to call together small groups for literature discussion. See pp. 124–128 for suggested trade book titles.

Independent

Options for Independent Work

- Independent Reading
- Letter/Word Study: Letter Sorting
- Vocabulary in Context Cards 37–42
- Listening Center: respond in Reader's Notebook
- Reader's Notebook: see writing prompt
- Ready-Made Work Stations, Lesson 7: Comprehension and Fluency, Word Study, Think and Write

See Teacher's Edition Lesson 7 for more independent activity options.

Writing About Reading

- Prompt: *How Animals Communicate* and *Insect Messages* both tell about animals. Draw or write about one of the animals you read about. Tell why you think it is interesting.
- Have children use their Reader's Notebook to record reactions to the literature they read and listened to this week.

GROUP SHARE Wrap up each day's Readers' Workshop by asking children to share how they applied the minilesson principle to their independent reading. Look for the Group Share section at the end of each minilesson.

Suggested Weekly Focus

Whole Group

Interactive Read-Aloud/ Shared Reading

- *A Musical Day* by Jerdine Nolan, Student Book: Lesson 8 REALISTIC FICTION
- *The Neighbors,* Teacher's Edition: Lesson 8 FOLKTALE
- *Drums* by Tim Pano, Student Book: Lesson 8 INFORMATIONAL TEXT

Whole-Group Links

You may use the suggested links to teach and reinforce skills in shared reading.

- *Review Short o* PHONICS
- *Clusters with l* PHONICS
- *Introduce Vocabulary (Vocabulary in Context Cards 43–48)* WORD STUDY
- *Classification/Categorization of Words: Time* VOCABULARY STRATEGIES

Reading Minilessons

- Sequence of Events: What Happens First and Next, p. 54
- Sequence of Events: The Order of What Happens, p. 55
- Diagram: Pictures and Labels, p. 55

Use the minilessons in this guide as a bridge between shared reading experiences and guided/ independent reading.

Small Group

Guided Reading

Select texts according to your children's instructional level. You may use the books below or select from the Leveled Readers Database, pp. 112–123. For instructional support, use the Leveled Readers Teacher's Guides along with the books that you choose.

- **LEVEL B** *Dress Up* REALISTIC FICTION
- **LEVEL C** *Music* (Vocabulary Reader) INFORMATIONAL TEXT
- **LEVEL D** *Nana's House* REALISTIC FICTION
- **LEVEL D** *Our Day at Nana's House* (Language Support) REALISTIC FICTION
- **LEVEL J** *The Beach* REALISTIC FICTION

For strategic intervention, use the Write-In Reader: *Hit It!*

Small-Group Links

- *Sequence of Events; Analyze/Evaluate* COMPREHENSION
- *Review Short o* PHONICS
- *Clusters with l* PHONICS
- *Phrasing: Natural Pauses* FLUENCY
- *Classification/Categorization of Words: Time* VOCABULARY STRATEGIES

Literature Discussion

You may want to call together small groups for literature discussion. See pp. 124–128 for suggested trade book titles.

Independent

Options for Independent Work

- Independent Reading
- Letter/Word Study: Letter Sorting
- Vocabulary in Context Cards 43–48
- Listening Center: respond in Reader's Notebook
- Reader's Notebook: see writing prompt
- Ready-Made Work Stations, Lesson 8: Comprehension and Fluency, Word Study, Think and Write

See Teacher's Edition Lesson 8 for more independent activity options.

Writing About Reading

- Prompt: *A Musical Day* is a story about children who make and play instruments. Draw and write about an instrument you would like to play.
- Have children use their Reader's Notebook to record reactions to the literature they read and listened to this week.

GROUP SHARE Wrap up each day's Readers' Workshop by asking children to share how they applied the minilesson principle to their independent reading. Look for the Group Share section at the end of each minilesson.

Whole Group

Interactive Read-Aloud/ Shared Reading

- *Dr. Seuss* by Helen Lester, Student Book: Lesson 9 BIOGRAPHY
- *The Little Red Hen*, Teacher's Edition: Lesson 9 FAIRY TALE
- *Two Poems from Dr. Seuss* by Dr. Seuss, Student Book: Lesson 9 POETRY

Whole-Group Links

You may use the suggested links to teach and reinforce skills in shared reading.

- *Review Short* e PHONICS
- *Clusters with* s PHONICS
- *Introduce Vocabulary (Vocabulary in Context Cards 49–54)* WORD STUDY
- *Antonyms* VOCABULARY STRATEGIES

Reading Minilessons

- Genre: Biography, p. 56
- Genre: Fairy Tale, p. 57
- Genre: Poetry, p. 57

Use the minilessons in this guide as a bridge between shared reading experiences and guided/ independent reading.

Small Group

Guided Reading

Select texts according to your children's instructional level. You may use the books below or select from the Leveled Readers Database, pp. 112–123. For instructional support, use the Leveled Readers Teacher's Guides along with the books that you choose.

- **LEVEL B** *Drawing* INFORMATIONAL TEXT
- **LEVEL C** *Reading Together* (Vocabulary Reader) INFORMATIONAL TEXT
- **LEVEL E** *Jim Henson, the Puppet Man* INFORMATIONAL TEXT
- **LEVEL E** *The Man Who Made Puppets* (Language Support) INFORMATIONAL TEXT
- **LEVEL J** *Margret and Hans Rey* INFORMATIONAL TEXT

For strategic intervention, use the Write-In Reader: *Scott and His Red Pen.*

Small-Group Links

- *Text and Graphic Features; Question* COMPREHENSION
- *Review Short* e PHONICS
- *Clusters with* s PHONICS
- *Accuracy: Word Recognition* FLUENCY
- *Antonyms* VOCABULARY STRATEGIES

Literature Discussion

You may want to call together small groups for literature discussion. See pp. 124–128 for suggested trade book titles.

Independent

Options for Independent Work

- Independent Reading
- Letter/Word Study: Letter Sorting
- Vocabulary in Context Cards 49–54
- Listening Center: respond in Reader's Notebook
- Reader's Notebook: see writing prompt
- Ready-Made Work Stations, Lesson 9: Comprehension and Fluency, Word Study, Think and Write

See Teacher's Edition Lesson 9 for more independent activity options.

Writing About Reading

- Prompt: If you could meet Dr. Seuss, what would you ask or tell him? Draw and write to explain.
- Have children use their Reader's Notebook to record reactions to the literature they read and listened to this week.

GROUP SHARE Wrap up each day's Readers' Workshop by asking children to share how they applied the minilesson principle to their independent reading. Look for the Group Share section at the end of each minilesson.

Suggested Weekly Focus

Whole Group

Interactive Read-Aloud/ Shared Reading

- *A Cupcake Party* by David McPhail, Student Book: Lesson 10 FANTASY
- *Chipper Chips In,* Teacher's Edition: Lesson 10 FANTASY
- *At the Bakery* by Kim Lee, Student Book: Lesson 10 READERS' THEATER

Whole-Group Links

You may use the suggested links to teach and reinforce skills in shared reading.

- *Review Short* u PHONICS
- *Final Clusters* PHONICS
- *Introduce Vocabulary (Vocabulary in Context Cards 55–60)* WORD STUDY
- *Synonyms* VOCABULARY STRATEGIES

Reading Minilessons

- Story Structure: How Characters Solve a Problem, p. 58
- Story Structure: Notice Characters' Problems, p. 59
- Directions: Notice Author's Explanation, p. 59

Use the minilessons in this guide as a bridge between shared reading experiences and guided/ independent reading.

Small Group

Guided Reading

Select texts according to your children's instructional level. You may use the books below or select from the Leveled Readers Database, pp. 112–123. For instructional support, use the Leveled Readers Teacher's Guides along with the books that you choose.

- **LEVEL B**   *Trip to the Rock* FANTASY
- **LEVEL C**   *Happy Birthday!* (Vocabulary Reader) INFORMATIONAL TEXT
- **LEVEL E**   *Happy Birthday, Toad* (Language Support) FANTASY
- **LEVEL E**   *Toad's Birthday* FANTASY
- **LEVEL I**   *Chipmunk's New Home* FANTASY

For strategic intervention, use the Write-In Reader: *Who Can Help Cat?*

Small-Group Links

- *Story Structure; Visualize* COMPREHENSION
- *Review Short* u PHONICS
- *Final Clusters* PHONICS
- *Stress* FLUENCY
- *Synonyms* VOCABULARY STRATEGIES

Literature Discussion

You may want to call together small groups for literature discussion. See pp. 124–128 for suggested trade book titles.

Independent

Options for Independent Work

- Independent Reading
- Letter/Word Study: Letter Sorting
- Vocabulary in Context Cards 55–60
- Listening Center: respond in Reader's Notebook
- Reader's Notebook: see writing prompt
- Ready-Made Work Stations, Lesson 10: Comprehension and Fluency, Word Study, Think and Write

See Teacher's Edition Lesson 10 for more independent activity options.

Writing About Reading

- Prompt: How are *A Cupcake Party* and *At the Bakery* the same? Draw and write to explain your ideas.
- Have children use their Reader's Notebook to record reactions to the literature they read and listened to this week.

GROUP SHARE Wrap up each day's Readers' Workshop by asking children to share how they applied the minilesson principle to their independent reading. Look for the Group Share section at the end of each minilesson.

Whole Group

Interactive Read-Aloud/ Shared Reading

- *Sea Animals* by Norbert Wu, Student Book: Lesson 11 INFORMATIONAL TEXT
- *The Piano Lessons*, Teacher's Edition: Lesson 11 REALISTIC FICTION
- *Water*, Student Book: Lesson 11 INFORMATIONAL TEXT

Whole-Group Links

You may use the suggested links to teach and reinforce skills in shared reading.

- *Digraph* th PHONICS
- *Base Words and* -s, -es, -ed, -ing PHONICS
- *Introduce Vocabulary (Vocabulary in Context Cards 61–68)* WORD STUDY
- *Classification/Categorization of Words: Colors* VOCABULARY STRATEGIES

Reading Minilessons

- Author's Purpose: To Inform, p. 60
- Author's Purpose: To Entertain, p. 61
- Genre: Informational Text, p. 61

Use the minilessons in this guide as a bridge between shared reading experiences and guided/ independent reading.

Small Group

Guided Reading

Select texts according to your children's instructional level. You may use the books below or select from the Leveled Readers Database, pp. 112–123. For instructional support, use the Leveled Readers Teacher's Guides along with the books that you choose.

- **LEVEL D** *In the Sea* INFORMATIONAL TEXT
- **LEVEL D** *Shark* (Vocabulary Reader) INFORMATIONAL TEXT
- **LEVEL G** *Life in the Coral Reefs* (Language Support) INFORMATIONAL TEXT
- **LEVEL H** *Coral Reefs* INFORMATIONAL TEXT
- **LEVEL L** *The Amazing Octopus* INFORMATIONAL TEXT

For strategic intervention, use the Write-In Reader: *Pup's Bath.*

Small-Group Links

- *Author's Purpose; Analyze/Evaluate* COMPREHENSION
- *Digraph* th PHONICS
- *Base Words and* -s, -es, -ed, -ing PHONICS
- *Phrasing: Attention to Punctuation (Comma)* FLUENCY
- *Classification/Categorization of Words: Colors* VOCABULARY STRATEGIES

Literature Discussion

You may want to call together small groups for literature discussion. See pp. 124–128 for suggested trade book titles.

Independent

Options for Independent Work

- Independent Reading
- Letter/Word Study: Letter Sorting
- Vocabulary in Context Cards 61–68
- Listening Center: respond in Reader's Notebook
- Reader's Notebook: see writing prompt
- Ready-Made Work Stations, Lesson 11: Comprehension and Fluency, Word Study, Think and Write

See Teacher's Edition Lesson 11 for more independent activity options.

Writing About Reading

- Prompt: Norbert Wu is the author and photographer of *Sea Animals*. Write him a note or draw a picture for him. Tell him how you feel about the book. Ask him questions.
- Have children use their Reader's Notebook to record reactions to the literature they read and listened to this week.

GROUP SHARE Wrap up each day's Readers' Workshop by asking children to share how they applied the minilesson principle to their independent reading. Look for the Group Share section at the end of each minilesson.

Suggested Weekly Focus

Whole Group

Interactive Read-Aloud/ Shared Reading

- *How Leopard Got His Spots* by Gerald McDermott, Student Book: Lesson 12 FOLKTALE
- *Turtle, Frog, and Rat,* Teacher's Edition: Lesson 12 FOLKTALE
- *The Rain Forest,* Student Book: Lesson 12 INFORMATIONAL TEXT

Whole-Group Links

You may use the suggested links to teach and reinforce skills in shared reading.

- *Digraphs* ch, tch PHONICS
- *Possessives* with 's PHONICS
- *Introduce Vocabulary (Vocabulary in Context Cards 69–76)* WORD STUDY
- *Homophones* VOCABULARY STRATEGIES

Reading Minilessons

- Sequence of Events: First, Next, and Last, p. 62
- Genre: Folktale, p. 63
- Genre: Informational Text, p. 63

Use the minilessons in this guide as a bridge between shared reading experiences and guided/ independent reading.

Small Group

Guided Reading

Select texts according to your children's instructional level. You may use the books below or select from the Leveled Readers Database, pp. 112–123. For instructional support, use the Leveled Readers Teacher's Guides along with the books that you choose.

- **LEVEL D** *Spots* (Vocabulary Reader) INFORMATIONAL TEXT
- **LEVEL E** *Giraffe's Neck* FOLKTALE
- **LEVEL H** *Bear's Long, Brown Tail* (Language Support) FOLKTALE
- **LEVEL H** *Bear's Tail* FOLKTALE
- **LEVEL L** *Peacock's Tail* FOLKTALE

For strategic intervention, use the Write-In Reader: *Al and Lop.*

Small-Group Links

- *Sequence of Events; Question* COMPREHENSION
- *Digraphs* ch, tch PHONICS
- *Possessives* with 's PHONICS
- *Rate* FLUENCY
- *Homophones* VOCABULARY STRATEGIES

Literature Discussion

You may want to call together small groups for literature discussion. See pp. 124–128 for suggested trade book titles.

Independent

Options for Independent Work

- Independent Reading
- Letter/Word Study: Letter Sorting
- Vocabulary in Context Cards 69–76
- Listening Center: respond in Reader's Notebook
- Reader's Notebook: see writing prompt
- Ready-Made Work Stations, Lesson 12: Comprehension and Fluency, Word Study, Think and Write

See Teacher's Edition Lesson 12 for more independent activity options.

Writing About Reading

- Prompt: How are the stories *How Leopard Got His Spots* and *Turtle, Frog, and Rat* the same? How are they different? Write or draw to show your ideas.
- Have children use their Reader's Notebook to record reactions to the literature they read and listened to this week.

GROUP SHARE Wrap up each day's Readers' Workshop by asking children to share how they applied the minilesson principle to their independent reading. Look for the Group Share section at the end of each minilesson.

Whole Group

Interactive Read-Aloud/ Shared Reading

- *Seasons* by Pat Cummings, Student Book: Lesson 13 INFORMATIONAL TEXT
- *The Prickly Pride of Texas,* Teacher's Edition: Lesson 13 INFORMATIONAL TEXT
- *The Four Seasons,* Student Book: Lesson 13 POETRY

Whole-Group Links

You may use the suggested links to teach and reinforce skills in shared reading.

- *Digraphs* sh, wh, ph PHONICS
- *Contractions with* 's, n't PHONICS
- *Introduce Vocabulary (Vocabulary in Context Cards 77–84)* WORD STUDY
- *Words Ending in* -ed, -ing, *or* -s VOCABULARY STRATEGIES

Reading Minilessons

- Cause and Effect: One Thing Makes Another Happen, p. 64
- Genre: Informational Text, p. 65
- Genre: Poetry, p. 65

Use the minilessons in this guide as a bridge between shared reading experiences and guided/ independent reading.

Small Group

Guided Reading

Select texts according to your children's instructional level. You may use the books below or select from the Leveled Readers Database, pp. 112–123. For instructional support, use the Leveled Readers Teacher's Guides along with the books that you choose.

- **LEVEL B** *Winter* INFORMATIONAL TEXT
- **LEVEL D** *Ducks* (Vocabulary Reader) INFORMATIONAL TEXT
- **LEVEL H** *In the Fall* (Language Support) INFORMATIONAL TEXT
- **LEVEL I** *Fall Changes* INFORMATIONAL TEXT
- **LEVEL K** *Seasons Around the World* INFORMATIONAL TEXT

For strategic intervention, use the Write-In Reader: *Max Has His Bath.*

Small-Group Links

- *Cause and Effect; Visualize* COMPREHENSION
- *Digraphs* sh, wh, ph PHONICS
- *Contractions with* 's, n't PHONICS
- *Accuracy: Word Recognition* FLUENCY
- *Words Ending in* -ed, -ing, *or* -s VOCABULARY STRATEGIES

Literature Discussion

You may want to call together small groups for literature discussion. See pp. 124–128 for suggested trade book titles.

Independent

Options for Independent Work

- Independent Reading
- Letter/Word Study: Letter Sorting
- Vocabulary in Context Cards 77–84
- Listening Center: respond in Reader's Notebook
- Reader's Notebook: see writing prompt
- Ready-Made Work Stations, Lesson 13: Comprehension and Fluency, Word Study, Think and Write

See Teacher's Edition Lesson 13 for more independent activity options.

Writing About Reading

- Prompt: Pick a season. Write and draw a postcard to a friend to tell about one thing you do in that season. Show and tell what the weather is like.
- Have children use their Reader's Notebook to record reactions to the literature they read and listened to this week.

GROUP SHARE Wrap up each day's Readers' Workshop by asking children to share how they applied the minilesson principle to their independent reading. Look for the Group Share section at the end of each minilesson.

Whole Group

Interactive Read-Aloud/ Shared Reading

- *The Big Race* by Pam Muñoz Ryan, Student Book: Lesson 14 FANTASY
- *The Tortoise and the Hare*, Teacher's Edition: Lesson 14 FABLE
- *The Olympic Games* by Margaret Bishop, Student Book: Lesson 14 INFORMATIONAL TEXT

Whole-Group Links

You may use the suggested links to teach and reinforce skills in shared reading.

- *Long* a *(CVCe); Phonogram* -ake PHONICS
- *Soft* c, g, dge; *Phonogram* -ace PHONICS
- *Introduce Vocabulary (Vocabulary in Context Cards 85–92)* WORD STUDY
- *Classification/Categorization of Words: Numbers* VOCABULARY STRATEGIES

Reading Minilessons

- Conclusions: Using Clues about Characters, p. 66
- Conclusions: Using What Characters Say and Do, p. 67
- Genre: Informational Text, p. 67

Use the minilessons in this guide as a bridge between shared reading experiences and guided/ independent reading.

Small Group

Guided Reading

Select texts according to your children's instructional level. You may use the books below or select from the Leveled Readers Database, pp. 112–123. For instructional support, use the Leveled Readers Teacher's Guides along with the books that you choose.

- **LEVEL D** *Izzy's Move* FANTASY
- **LEVEL E** *Desert Animals* (Vocabulary Reader) INFORMATIONAL TEXT
- **LEVEL I** *The Map and the Treasure* (Language Support) FANTASY
- **LEVEL I** *The Treasure Map* FANTASY
- **LEVEL K** *Cam the Camel* FANTASY

For strategic intervention, use the Write-In Reader: *Jake's Best Race.*

Small-Group Links

- *Conclusions; Infer/Predict* COMPREHENSION
- *Long* a *(CVCe); Phonogram* -ake PHONICS
- *Soft* c, g, dge; *Phonogram* -ace PHONICS
- *Expression* FLUENCY
- *Classification/Categorization of Words: Numbers* VOCABULARY STRATEGIES

Literature Discussion

You may want to call together small groups for literature discussion. See pp. 124–128 for suggested trade book titles.

Independent

Options for Independent Work

- Independent Reading
- Letter/Word Study: Letter Sorting
- Vocabulary in Context Cards 85–92
- Listening Center: respond in Reader's Notebook
- Reader's Notebook: see writing prompt
- Ready-Made Work Stations, Lesson 14: Comprehension and Fluency, Word Study, Think and Write

See Teacher's Edition Lesson 14 for more independent activity options.

Writing About Reading

- Prompt: Imagine you are the coach for one of the characters or athletes you read about this week. Write or draw to tell what you would say or do to help him or her.
- Have children use their Reader's Notebook to record reactions to the literature they read and listened to this week.

GROUP SHARE Wrap up each day's Readers' Workshop by asking children to share how they applied the minilesson principle to their independent reading. Look for the Group Share section at the end of each minilesson.

Whole Group

Interactive Read-Aloud/ Shared Reading

- *Animal Groups* by James Bruchac, Student Book: Lesson 15 INFORMATIONAL TEXT
- *The Dancing Wolves,* Teacher's Edition: Lesson 15 FANTASY
- *Animal Picnic* by Debbie O'Brien, Student Book: Lesson 15 READERS' THEATER

Whole-Group Links

You may use the suggested links to teach and reinforce skills in shared reading.

- *Long* i (*CVC*e) PHONICS
- *Digraphs* kn, wr, gn, mb PHONICS
- *Introduce Vocabulary (Vocabulary in Context Cards 93–100)* WORD STUDY
- *Suffixes* -er, -est VOCABULARY STRATEGIES

Reading Minilessons

- Compare and Contrast: How Things are the Same and Different, p. 68
- Story Structure: What Happened and What Happens Next, p. 69
- Compare and Contrast: How Characters are the Same and Different, p. 69

Use the minilessons in this guide as a bridge between shared reading experiences and guided/ independent reading.

Small Group

Guided Reading

Select texts according to your children's instructional level. You may use the books below or select from the Leveled Readers Database, pp. 112–123. For instructional support, use the Leveled Readers Teacher's Guides along with the books that you choose.

- **LEVEL D** *Making a Home* INFORMATIONAL TEXT
- **LEVEL E** *Animals* (Vocabulary Reader) INFORMATIONAL TEXT
- **LEVEL J** *All About Bats* INFORMATIONAL TEXT
- **LEVEL J** *Many Kinds of Bats* (Language Support) INFORMATIONAL TEXT
- **LEVEL L** *Bald Eagles* INFORMATIONAL TEXT

For strategic intervention, use the Write-In Reader: *Cats.*

Small-Group Links

- *Compare and Contrast; Monitor/Clarify* COMPREHENSION
- *Long* i (*CVC*e) PHONICS
- *Digraphs* kn, wr, gn, mb PHONICS
- *Intonation* FLUENCY
- *Suffixes* -er, -est VOCABULARY STRATEGIES

Literature Discussion

You may want to call together small groups for literature discussion. See pp. 124–128 for suggested trade book titles.

Independent

Options for Independent Work

- Independent Reading
- Letter/Word Study: Letter Sorting
- Vocabulary in Context Cards 93–100
- Listening Center: respond in Reader's Notebook
- Reader's Notebook: see writing prompt
- Ready-Made Work Stations, Lesson 15: Comprehension and Fluency, Word Study, Think and Write

See Teacher's Edition Lesson 15 for more independent activity options.

Writing About Reading

- Prompt: Draw an animal you like. Label the picture with the name of the animal group it belongs to. Label its body parts. List other things that make it part of the group.
- Have children use their Reader's Notebook to record reactions to the literature they read and listened to this week.

GROUP SHARE Wrap up each day's Readers' Workshop by asking children to share how they applied the minilesson principle to their independent reading. Look for the Group Share section at the end of each minilesson.

Suggested Weekly Focus

Whole Group

Interactive Read-Aloud/ Shared Reading

- *Let's Go to the Moon!* by Stephen R. Swinburne, Student Book: Lesson 16 INFORMATIONAL TEXT
- *One Giant Leap,* Teacher's Edition: Lesson 16 INFORMATIONAL TEXT
- *Mae Jemison* by Debbie O'Brien, Student Book: Lesson 16 BIOGRAPHY

Whole-Group Links

You may use the suggested links to teach and reinforce skills in shared reading.

- *Long* o *(CV, CVCe)* PHONICS
- *Long* u *(CVCe)* PHONICS
- *Introduce Vocabulary (Vocabulary in Context Cards 101–108)* WORD STUDY
- *Suffixes* -y, -ful VOCABULARY STRATEGIES

Reading Minilessons

- Main Idea and Details: Author's Focus, p. 70
- Main Idea and Details: Book's Main Idea, p. 71
- Genre: Biography, p. 71

Use the minilessons in this guide as a bridge between shared reading experiences and guided/ independent reading.

Small Group

Guided Reading

Select texts according to your children's instructional level. You may use the books below or select from the Leveled Readers Database, pp. 112–123. For instructional support, use the Leveled Readers Teacher's Guides along with the books that you choose.

- **LEVEL D** *In the Sky* (Vocabulary Reader) INFORMATIONAL TEXT
- **LEVEL D** *The Sun* INFORMATIONAL TEXT
- **LEVEL I** *Seasons* INFORMATIONAL TEXT TEXT
- **LEVEL I** *The Seasons of the Year* (Language Support) INFORMATIONAL TEXT
- **LEVEL J** *Living and Working in Space* INFORMATIONAL TEXT

For strategic intervention, use the Write-In Reader: *Bo's Big Space Trip.*

Small-Group Links

- *Main Idea and Details; Question* COMPREHENSION
- *Long* o *(CV, CVCe)* PHONICS
- *Long* u *(CVCe)* PHONICS
- *Stress* FLUENCY
- *Suffixes* -y, -ful VOCABULARY STRATEGIES

Literature Discussion

You may want to call together small groups for literature discussion. See pp. 124–128 for suggested trade book titles.

Independent

Options for Independent Work

- Independent Reading
- Word Study
- Vocabulary in Context Cards 101–108
- Listening Center: respond in Reader's Notebook
- Reader's Notebook: see writing prompt
- Ready-Made Work Stations, Lesson 16: Comprehension and Fluency, Word Study, Think and Write

See Teacher's Edition Lesson 16 for more independent activity options.

Writing About Reading

- Prompt: *Let's Go to the Moon!* tells about the Moon and things that astronauts did there. Draw or write about something you learned about the Moon that you did not know before.
- Have children use their Reader's Notebook to record reactions to the literature they read and listened to this week.

GROUP SHARE Wrap up each day's Readers' Workshop by asking children to share how they applied the minilesson principle to their independent reading. Look for the Group Share section at the end of each minilesson.

Whole Group

Interactive Read-Aloud/ Shared Reading

- *The Big Trip* by Valeri Gorbachev, Student Book: Lesson 17 FANTASY
- *The Rainy Trip*, Teacher's Edition: Lesson 17 REALISTIC FICTION
- *Lewis and Clark's Big Trip*, Student Book: Lesson 17 INFORMATIONAL TEXT

Whole-Group Links

You may use the suggested links to teach and reinforce skills in shared reading.

- *Long* e *(CV, CVCe); Vowel Pairs* ee, ea PHONICS
- *Final* ng, nk PHONICS
- *Introduce Vocabulary (Vocabulary in Context Cards 109–116)* WORD STUDY
- *Classification/Categorization of Words: Transportation* VOCABULARY STRATEGIES

Reading Minilessons

- Compare and Contrast: Things in a Story, p. 72
- Compare and Contrast: Beginning and End of a Story, p. 73
- Genre: Informational Text, p. 73

Use the minilessons in this guide as a bridge between shared reading experiences and guided/ independent reading.

Small Group

Guided Reading

Select texts according to your children's instructional level. You may use the books below or select from the Leveled Readers Database, pp. 112–123. For instructional support, use the Leveled Readers Teacher's Guides along with the books that you choose.

- **LEVEL E** *Bear Swims* FANTASY
- **LEVEL E** *Going to School* (Vocabulary Reader) INFORMATIONAL TEXT
- **LEVEL H** *Flying* FANTASY
- **LEVEL H** *Flying in an Airplane* (Language Support) FANTASY
- **LEVEL J** *The Mountain* FANTASY

For strategic intervention, use the Write-In Reader: *Pops Takes a Trip*.

Small-Group Links

- *Compare and Contrast; Visualize* COMPREHENSION
- *Long* e *(CV, CVCe); Vowel Pairs* ee, ea PHONICS
- *Final* ng, nk PHONICS
- *Phrasing: Attention to Punctuation (Question Mark)* FLUENCY
- *Classification/Categorization of Words: Transportation* VOCABULARY STRATEGIES

Literature Discussion

You may want to call together small groups for literature discussion. See pp. 124–128 for suggested trade book titles.

Independent

Options for Independent Work

- Independent Reading
- Word Study
- Vocabulary in Context Cards 109–116
- Listening Center: respond in Reader's Notebook
- Reader's Notebook: see writing prompt
- Ready-Made Work Stations, Lesson 17: Comprehension and Fluency, Word Study, Think and Write

See Teacher's Edition Lesson 17 for more independent activity options.

Writing About Reading

- Prompt: *The Big Trip* and *Lewis and Clark's Big Trip* both tell about trips. Draw or write one way they are the same. Draw or write one way they are different.
- Have children use their Reader's Notebook to record reactions to the literature they read and listened to this week.

GROUP SHARE Wrap up each day's Readers' Workshop by asking children to share how they applied the minilesson principle to their independent reading. Look for the Group Share section at the end of each minilesson.

Whole Group

Interactive Read-Aloud/ Shared Reading

- *Where Does Food Come From?* by Shelley Rotner, Student Book: Lesson 18 INFORMATIONAL TEXT
- *The Three Wishes*, Teacher's Edition: Lesson 18 FAIRY TALE
- *Jack and the Beanstalk*, Student Book: Lesson 18 FAIRY TALE

Whole-Group Links

You may use the suggested links to teach and reinforce skills in shared reading.

- *Vowel Pairs* ai, ay PHONICS
- *Contractions* 'll, 'd PHONICS
- *Introduce Vocabulary (Vocabulary in Context Cards 117–124)* WORD STUDY
- *Multiple-Meaning Words* VOCABULARY STRATEGIES

Reading Minilessons

- Author's Purpose: What You Can Learn, p. 74
- Genre: Fairy Tale, p. 75
- Genre: Fairy Tale, p. 75

Use the minilessons in this guide as a bridge between shared reading experiences and guided/ independent reading.

Small Group

Guided Reading

Select texts according to your children's instructional level. You may use the books below or select from the Leveled Readers Database, pp. 112–123. For instructional support, use the Leveled Readers Teacher's Guides along with the books that you choose.

- **LEVEL D** *Apples* INFORMATIONAL TEXT
- **LEVEL D** *My Favorite Foods* (Vocabulary Reader) INFORMATIONAL TEXT
- **LEVEL G** *How We Get Food* (Language Support) INFORMATIONAL TEXT
- **LEVEL H** *Food for You* INFORMATIONAL TEXT
- **LEVEL K** *A World of Food* INFORMATIONAL TEXT

For strategic intervention, use the Write-In Reader: *Ant's Grand Feast.*

Small-Group Links

- *Author's Purpose; Summarize* COMPREHENSION
- *Vowel Pairs* ai, ay PHONICS
- *Contractions* 'll, 'd PHONICS
- *Expression* FLUENCY
- *Multiple-Meaning Words* VOCABULARY STRATEGIES

Literature Discussion

You may want to call together small groups for literature discussion. See pp. 124–128 for suggested trade book titles.

Independent

Options for Independent Work

- Independent Reading
- Word Study
- Vocabulary in Context Cards 117–124
- Listening Center: respond in Reader's Notebook
- Reader's Notebook: see writing prompt
- Ready-Made Work Stations, Lesson 18: Comprehension and Fluency, Word Study, Think and Write

See Teacher's Edition Lesson 18 for more independent activity options.

Writing About Reading

- Prompt: At the end of *Jack and the Beanstalk*, Jack cuts down the beanstalk. He and his mother live happily ever after with their goose. How would you write the story with a different ending? Draw or write your new ending to the story.
- Have children use their Reader's Notebook to record reactions to the literature they read and listened to this week.

GROUP SHARE Wrap up each day's Readers' Workshop by asking children to share how they applied the minilesson principle to their independent reading. Look for the Group Share section at the end of each minilesson.

Whole Group

Interactive Read-Aloud/Shared Reading

- *Tomás Rivera* by Jane Medina, Student Book: Lesson 19 BIOGRAPHY
- *Christina's Work*, Teacher's Edition: Lesson 19 BIOGRAPHY
- *Life Then and Now,* Student Book: Lesson 19 INFORMATIONAL TEXT

Whole-Group Links

You may use the suggested links to teach and reinforce skills in shared reading.

- *Vowel Pairs* oa, ow PHONICS
- *Contractions* 've, 're PHONICS
- *Introduce Vocabulary (Vocabulary in Context Cards 125–132)* WORD STUDY
- *Synonyms* VOCABULARY STRATEGIES

Reading Minilessons

- Conclusions: What Story Characters Do, p. 76
- Conclusions: Information About the Subject, p. 77
- Compare and Contrast: Same and Different, p. 77

Use the minilessons in this guide as a bridge between shared reading experiences and guided/ independent reading.

Small Group

Guided Reading

Select texts according to your children's instructional level. You may use the books below or select from the Leveled Readers Database, pp. 112–123. For instructional support, use the Leveled Readers Teacher's Guides along with the books that you choose.

- **LEVEL D** *People in the Town* (Vocabulary Reader) INFORMATIONAL TEXT
- **LEVEL E** *Working in the Park* REALISTIC FICTION
- **LEVEL H** *Our Bakery* REALISTIC FICTION
- **LEVEL H** *Our Day at the Bakery* (Language Support) REALISTIC FICTION
- **LEVEL J** *What I Want to Be* REALISTIC FICTION

For strategic intervention, use the Write-In Reader: *When Tom Grows Up.*

Small-Group Links

- *Conclusions; Monitor/Clarify* COMPREHENSION
- *Vowel Pairs* oa, ow PHONICS
- *Contractions* 've, 're PHONICS
- *Intonation* FLUENCY
- *Synonyms* VOCABULARY STRATEGIES

Literature Discussion

You may want to call together small groups for literature discussion. See pp. 124–128 for suggested trade book titles.

Independent

Options for Independent Work

- Independent Reading
- Word Study
- Vocabulary in Context Cards 125–132
- Listening Center: respond in Reader's Notebook
- Reader's Notebook: see writing prompt
- Ready-Made Work Stations, Lesson 19: Comprehension and Fluency, Word Study, Think and Write

See Teacher's Edition Lesson 19 for more independent activity options.

Writing About Reading

- *Tomás Rivera* tells about some important events in Tomás Rivera's life. Draw or write to tell about those events in the order they happened.
- Have children use their Reader's Notebook to record reactions to the literature they read and listened to this week.

GROUP SHARE Wrap up each day's Readers' Workshop by asking children to share how they applied the minilesson principle to their independent reading. Look for the Group Share section at the end of each minilesson.

Whole Group

Interactive Read-Aloud/ Shared Reading

- *Little Rabbit's Tale* by Wong Herbert Yee, Student Book: Lesson 20 FOLKTALE
- *Chicken Little,* Teacher's Edition: Lesson 20 FOLKTALE
- *Silly Poems,* Student Book: Lesson 20 POETRY

Whole-Group Links

You may use the suggested links to teach and reinforce skills in shared reading.

- *Compound Words* PHONICS
- *Short Vowel /e/ea* PHONICS
- *Introduce Vocabulary (Vocabulary in Context Cards 133–140)* WORD STUDY
- *Compound Words* VOCABULARY STRATEGIES

Reading Minilessons

- Cause and Effect: How One Thing Makes Other Things Happen, p. 78
- Genre: Folktale, p. 79
- Genre: Poetry, p. 79

Use the minilessons in this guide as a bridge between shared reading experiences and guided/ independent reading.

Small Group

Guided Reading

Select texts according to your children's instructional level. You may use the books below or select from the Leveled Readers Database, pp. 112–123. For instructional support, use the Leveled Readers Teacher's Guides along with the books that you choose.

- **LEVEL D** *Putting Frosting on the Cake* FANTASY
- **LEVEL E** *The Weather* (Vocabulary Reader) INFORMATIONAL TEXT
- **LEVEL G** *Polly's Pet Polar Bear* (Language Support) FANTASY
- **LEVEL H** *Polar Bear Pete* FANTASY
- **LEVEL J** *Bobcat Tells a Tale* FANTASY

For strategic intervention, use the Write-In Reader: *Tree Frog Sings His Song.*

Small-Group Links

- *Cause and Effect; Infer/ Predict* COMPREHENSION
- *Compound Words* PHONICS
- *Short Vowel /e/ea* PHONICS
- *Rate* FLUENCY
- *Compound Words* VOCABULARY STRATEGIES

Literature Discussion

You may want to call together small groups for literature discussion. See pp. 124–128 for suggested trade book titles.

Independent

Options for Independent Work

- Independent Reading
- Word Study
- Vocabulary in Context Cards 133–140
- Listening Center: respond in Reader's Notebook
- Reader's Notebook: see writing prompt
- Ready-Made Work Stations, Lesson 20: Comprehension and Fluency, Word Study, Think and Write

See Teacher's Edition Lesson 20 for more independent activity options.

Writing About Reading

- Prompt: In *Silly Poems,* you read two poems. Which one did you like better? Draw or write to tell why you liked the poem that you did.
- Have children use their Reader's Notebook to record reactions to the literature they read and listened to this week.

GROUP SHARE Wrap up each day's Readers' Workshop by asking children to share how they applied the minilesson principle to their independent reading. Look for the Group Share section at the end of each minilesson.

Whole Group

Interactive Read-Aloud/ Shared Reading

- *The Tree* by Cynthia Rylant, Student Book: Lesson 21 FANTASY
- *Grandpa's Tree,* Teacher's Edition: Lesson 21 REALISTIC FICTION
- *It Comes from Trees* by Russ Andrew, Student Book: Lesson 21 INFORMATIONAL TEXT

Whole-Group Links

You may use the suggested links to teach and reinforce skills in shared reading.

- r-*Controlled Vowel* ar PHONICS
- r-*Controlled Vowels* or, ore PHONICS
- *Introduce Vocabulary (Vocabulary in Context Cards 141–148)* WORD STUDY
- *Prefix* re- VOCABULARY STRATEGIES

Reading Minilessons

- Story Structure: Problem and Solution, p. 80
- Story Structure: How Characters Work Together, p. 81
- Genre: Informational Text, p. 81

Use the minilessons in this guide as a bridge between shared reading experiences and guided/ independent reading.

Small Group

Guided Reading

Select texts according to your children's instructional level. You may use the books below or select from the Leveled Readers Database, pp. 112–123. For instructional support, use the Leveled Readers Teacher's Guides along with the books that you choose.

- **LEVEL E** *A Seed for Sid* FANTASY
- **LEVEL G** *Skunk Cooks Soup* (Language Support) FANTASY
- **LEVEL G** *Trees* (Vocabulary Reader) INFORMATIONAL TEXT
- **LEVEL H** *Forest Stew* FANTASY
- **LEVEL J** *Lena's Garden* FANTASY

For strategic intervention, use the Write-In Reader: *321 Park Street.*

Small-Group Links

- *Story Structure; Analyze/ Evaluate* COMPREHENSION
- r-*Controlled Vowel* ar PHONICS
- r-*Controlled Vowels* or, ore PHONICS
- *Phrasing: Natural Pauses* FLUENCY
- *Prefix* re- VOCABULARY STRATEGIES

Literature Discussion

You may want to call together small groups for literature discussion. See pp. 124–128 for suggested trade book titles.

Independent

Options for Independent Work

- Independent Reading
- Word Study
- Vocabulary in Context Cards 141–148
- Listening Center: respond in Reader's Notebook
- Reader's Notebook: see writing prompt
- Ready-Made Work Stations, Lesson 21: Comprehension and Fluency, Word Study, Think and Write

See Teacher's Edition Lesson 21 for more independent activity options.

Writing About Reading

- Prompt: In *The Tree,* Poppleton asked his animal friends what his tree needed. Imagine that Poppleton talked to more animals before talking to Cherry Sue. What might those animals think the tree needed? Write about what might have happened.
- Have children use their Reader's Notebook to record reactions to the literature they read and listened to this week.

GROUP SHARE Wrap up each day's Readers' Workshop by asking children to share how they applied the minilesson principle to their independent reading. Look for the Group Share section at the end of each minilesson.

Suggested Weekly Focus

Whole Group

Interactive Read-Aloud/ Shared Reading

- *Amazing Animals* by Gwendolyn Hooks, Student Book: Lesson 22 INFORMATIONAL TEXT
- *How Bat Learned to Fly*, Teacher's Edition: Lesson 22 FOLKTALE
- *The Ugly Duckling*, Student Book: Lesson 22 FAIRY TALE

Whole-Group Links

You may use the suggested links to teach and reinforce skills in shared reading.

- *r-Controlled Vowels* er, ir, ur PHONICS
- *Introduce Vocabulary (Vocabulary in Context Cards 149–156)* WORD STUDY
- *Using a Dictionary Entry* VOCABULARY STRATEGIES

Reading Minilessons

- Conclusions: Using What You Already Know, p. 82
- Conclusions: How Characters Feel, p. 83
- Genre: Fairy Tale, p. 83

Use the minilessons in this guide as a bridge between shared reading experiences and guided/ independent reading.

Small Group

Guided Reading

Select texts according to your children's instructional level. You may use the books below or select from the Leveled Readers Database, pp. 112–123. For instructional support, use the Leveled Readers Teacher's Guides along with the books that you choose.

- **LEVEL E** *Animal Homes* INFORMATIONAL TEXT
- **LEVEL E** *Baby Birds* (Vocabulary Reader) INFORMATIONAL TEXT
- **LEVEL I** *Baby Kangaroos* INFORMATIONAL TEXT
- **LEVEL I** *Tiny Baby Kangaroos* (Language Support) INFORMATIONAL TEXT
- **LEVEL J** *How Animals Move* INFORMATIONAL TEXT

For strategic intervention, use the Write-In Reader: *Peacock and Crane.*

Small-Group Links

- *Conclusions; Visualize* COMPREHENSION
- *r-Controlled Vowels* er, ir, ur PHONICS
- *Accuracy: Connected Text* FLUENCY
- *Using a Dictionary Entry* VOCABULARY STRATEGIES

Literature Discussion

You may want to call together small groups for literature discussion. See pp. 124–128 for suggested trade book titles.

Independent

Options for Independent Work

- Independent Reading
- Word Study
- Vocabulary in Context Cards 149–156
- Listening Center: respond in Reader's Notebook
- Reader's Notebook: see writing prompt
- Ready-Made Work Stations, Lesson 22: Comprehension and Fluency, Word Study, Think and Write

See Teacher's Edition Lesson 22 for more independent activity options.

Writing About Reading

- Prompt: *How Bat Learned to Fly* tells an idea about how something in nature came to be. What other things in nature could be explained in a story? Write a story about how this thing came to be.
- Have children use their Reader's Notebook to record reactions to the literature they read and listened to this week.

GROUP SHARE Wrap up each day's Readers' Workshop by asking children to share how they applied the minilesson principle to their independent reading. Look for the Group Share section at the end of each minilesson.

Whole Group

Interactive Read-Aloud/ Shared Reading

- *Whistle for Willie* by Ezra Jack Keats, Student Book: Lesson 23 REALISTIC FICTION
- *Around the World in a Day,* Teacher's Edition: Lesson 23 REALISTIC FICTION
- *Pet Poems,* Student Book: Lesson 23 POETRY

Whole-Group Links

You may use the suggested links to teach and reinforce skills in shared reading.

- *Vowel Digraph* oo PHONICS
- *Syllable Pattern (CVC)* PHONICS
- *Introduce Vocabulary (Vocabulary in Context Cards 157–164)* WORD STUDY
- *Classification/Categorization of Words: Family* VOCABULARY STRATEGIES

Reading Minilessons

- Cause and Effect: One Thing Makes Another Happen, p. 84
- Genre: Realistic Fiction, p. 85
- Genre: Poetry, p. 85

Use the minilessons in this guide as a bridge between shared reading experiences and guided/ independent reading.

Small Group

Guided Reading

Select texts according to your children's instructional level. You may use the books below or select from the Leveled Readers Database, pp. 112–123. For instructional support, use the Leveled Readers Teacher's Guides along with the books that you choose.

- **LEVEL E** *Amy's Airplane* REALISTIC FICTION
- **LEVEL F** *So Many Sounds* (Vocabulary Reader) INFORMATIONAL TEXT
- **LEVEL I** *Len's Tomato Plant* (Language Support) REALISTIC FICTION
- **LEVEL I** *Len's Tomatoes* REALISTIC FICTION
- **LEVEL L** *The Lemonade Stand* REALISTIC FICTION

For strategic intervention, use the Write-In Reader: *Pet Dreams.*

Small-Group Links

- *Cause and Effect; Monitor/Clarify* COMPREHENSION
- *Vowel Digraph* oo PHONICS
- *Syllable Pattern (CVC)* PHONICS
- *Stress* FLUENCY
- *Classification/Categorization of Words: Family* VOCABULARY STRATEGIES

Literature Discussion

You may want to call together small groups for literature discussion. See pp. 124–128 for suggested trade book titles.

Independent

Options for Independent Work

- Independent Reading
- Word Study
- Vocabulary in Context Cards 157–164
- Listening Center: respond in Reader's Notebook
- Reader's Notebook: see writing prompt
- Ready-Made Work Stations, Lesson 23: Comprehension and Fluency, Word Study, Think and Write

See Teacher's Edition Lesson 23 for more independent activity options.

Writing About Reading

- Prompt: *Whistle for Willie* tells about a boy named Peter who learns how to whistle. Draw or write about a time you learned to do something new.
- Have children use their Reader's Notebook to record reactions to the literature they read and listened to this week.

GROUP SHARE Wrap up each day's Readers' Workshop by asking children to share how they applied the minilesson principle to their independent reading. Look for the Group Share section at the end of each minilesson.

Suggested Weekly Focus

Whole Group

Interactive Read-Aloud/ Shared Reading

- *A Butterfly Grows* by Steve Swinburne, Student Book: Lesson 24 NARRATIVE NONFICTION
- *Visiting Butterflies*, Teacher's Edition: Lesson 24 INFORMATIONAL TEXT
- *Best Friends* by Stephen Gill, Student Book: Lesson 24 READERS' THEATER

Whole-Group Links

You may use the suggested links to teach and reinforce skills in shared reading.

- *Vowel Digraphs/Spelling Patterns:* oo, ou, ew PHONICS
- *More Spellings for /o͞o/:* ue, u, u_e PHONICS
- *Introduce Vocabulary (Vocabulary in Context Cards 165–172)* WORD STUDY
- *Multiple-Meaning Words* VOCABULARY STRATEGIES

Reading Minilessons

- Sequence of Events: How Things Grow and Change, p. 86
- Sequence of Events: First, Next, and Last, p. 87
- Genre: Play, p. 87

Use the minilessons in this guide as a bridge between shared reading experiences and guided/ independent reading.

Small Group

Guided Reading

Select texts according to your children's instructional level. You may use the books below or select from the Leveled Readers Database, pp. 112–123. For instructional support, use the Leveled Readers Teacher's Guides along with the books that you choose.

- **LEVEL F** *Butterflies* (Vocabulary Reader) INFORMATIONAL TEXT
- **LEVEL F** *Ladybugs* INFORMATIONAL TEXT
- **LEVEL I** *All About Fireflies* (Language Support) INFORMATIONAL TEXT
- **LEVEL I** *Fireflies* INFORMATIONAL TEXT
- **LEVEL L** *Honeybees* INFORMATIONAL TEXT

For strategic intervention, use the Write-In Reader: *The Things You Can Find.*

Small-Group Links

- *Sequence of Events; Question* COMPREHENSION
- *Vowel Digraphs/Spelling Patterns:* oo, ou, ew PHONICS
- *More Spellings for /o͞o/:* ue, u, u_e PHONICS
- *Expression* FLUENCY
- *Multiple-Meaning Words* VOCABULARY STRATEGIES

Literature Discussion

You may want to call together small groups for literature discussion. See pp. 124–128 for suggested trade book titles.

Independent

Options for Independent Work

- Independent Reading
- Word Study
- Vocabulary in Context Cards 165–172
- Listening Center: respond in Reader's Notebook
- Reader's Notebook: see writing prompt
- Ready-Made Work Stations, Lesson 24: Comprehension and Fluency, Word Study, Think and Write

See Teacher's Edition Lesson 24 for more independent activity options.

Writing About Reading

- Prompt: *A Butterfly Grows* tells how a butterfly grows and changes in its life. Draw and write to show and tell how a butterfly changes and grows.
- Have children use their Reader's Notebook to record reactions to the literature they read and listened to this week.

GROUP SHARE Wrap up each day's Readers' Workshop by asking children to share how they applied the minilesson principle to their independent reading. Look for the Group Share section at the end of each minilesson.

Whole Group

Interactive Read-Aloud/ Shared Reading

- *The New Friend* by María Puncel, Student Book: Lesson 25 REALISTIC FICTION
- *Señor Coyote, the Judge,* Teacher's Edition: Lesson 25 FOLKTALE
- *Neighborhoods* by Isabel Collins, Student Book: Lesson 25 INFORMATIONAL TEXT

Whole-Group Links

You may use the suggested links to teach and reinforce skills in shared reading.

- *Vowel Combinations* ou, ow PHONICS
- *Vowel Combinations* oi, oy, au, aw PHONICS
- *Introduce Vocabulary (Vocabulary in Context Cards 173–180)* WORD STUDY
- *Synonyms with Introduction to Thesaurus* VOCABULARY STRATEGIES

Reading Minilessons

- Understanding Characters: How Characters Are Like Real People, p. 88
- Understanding Characters: What Characters Do, p. 89
- Genre: Informational Text, p. 89

Use the minilessons in this guide as a bridge between shared reading experiences and guided/ independent reading.

Small Group

Guided Reading

Select texts according to your children's instructional level. You may use the books below or select from the Leveled Readers Database, pp. 112–123. For instructional support, use the Leveled Readers Teacher's Guides along with the books that you choose.

- **LEVEL F** *Molly's New Team* REALISTIC FICTION
- **LEVEL G** *Moving* (Vocabulary Reader) INFORMATIONAL TEXT
- **LEVEL H** *First Day of Second Grade* (Language Support) REALISTIC FICTION
- **LEVEL I** *Ready for Second Grade* REALISTIC FICTION
- **LEVEL J** *Tag-Along Tim* REALISTIC FICTION

For strategic intervention, use the Write-In Reader: *Who Will It Be?*

Small-Group Links

- *Understanding Characters; Summarize* COMPREHENSION
- *Vowel Combinations* ou, ow PHONICS
- *Vowel Combinations* oi, oy, au, aw PHONICS
- *Phrasing: Attention to Punctuation* FLUENCY
- *Synonyms with Introduction to Thesaurus* VOCABULARY STRATEGIES

Literature Discussion

You may want to call together small groups for literature discussion. See pp. 124–128 for suggested trade book titles.

Independent

Options for Independent Work

- Independent Reading
- Word Study
- Vocabulary in Context Cards 173–180
- Listening Center: respond in Reader's Notebook
- Reader's Notebook: see writing prompt
- Ready-Made Work Stations, Lesson 25: Comprehension and Fluency, Word Study, Think and Write

See Teacher's Edition Lesson 25 for more independent activity options.

Writing About Reading

- Prompt: *The New Friend* tells about some boys who welcome a new boy to their neighborhood. How would you welcome a new friend to your neighborhood? Draw and write to show and tell your ideas.
- Have children use their Reader's Notebook to record reactions to the literature they read and listened to this week.

GROUP SHARE Wrap up each day's Readers' Workshop by asking children to share how they applied the minilesson principle to their independent reading. Look for the Group Share section at the end of each minilesson.

Whole Group

Interactive Read-Aloud/ Shared Reading

- *The Dot* by Peter H. Reynolds, Student Book: Lesson 26 REALISTIC FICTION
- *The Art Contest,* Teacher's Edition: Lesson 26 REALISTIC FICTION
- *Artists Create Art!* by Anne Rogers, Student Book: Lesson 26 BIOGRAPHY

Whole-Group Links

You may use the suggested links to teach and reinforce skills in shared reading.

- *Base Words/Inflections* -ed, -ing *(CVCe, CVC)* PHONICS
- *Long* e *Spelling Patterns* y, ie PHONICS
- *Introduce Vocabulary (Vocabulary in Context Cards 181–188)* WORD STUDY
- *Figurative Language (Idioms)* VOCABULARY STRATEGIES

Reading Minilessons

- Compare and Contrast: Characters' Feelings, p. 90
- Compare and Contrast: Characters in Different Stories, p. 91
- Genre: Biography, p. 91

Use the minilessons in this guide as a bridge between shared reading experiences and guided/ independent reading.

Small Group

Guided Reading

Select texts according to your children's instructional level. You may use the books below or select from the Leveled Readers Database, pp. 112–123. For instructional support, use the Leveled Readers Teacher's Guides along with the books that you choose.

- **LEVEL F** *Our School* REALISTIC FICTION
- **LEVEL H** *The Bumpy Snowman* (Language Support) REALISTIC FICTION
- **LEVEL H** *Kamala's Art* (Vocabulary Reader) INFORMATIONAL TEXT
- **LEVEL I** *Paco's Snowman* REALISTIC FICTION
- **LEVEL J** *A Surprise for Ms. Green* REALISTIC FICTION

For strategic intervention, use the Write-In Reader: *Dog-Print Art.*

Small-Group Links

- *Compare and Contrast; Monitor/ Clarify* COMPREHENSION
- *Base Words/Inflections* -ed, -ing *(CVCe, CVC)* PHONICS
- *Long* e *Spelling Patterns* y, ie PHONICS
- *Accuracy: Self-Correct* FLUENCY
- *Figurative Language (Idioms)* VOCABULARY STRATEGIES

Literature Discussion

You may want to call together small groups for literature discussion. See pp. 124–128 for suggested trade book titles.

Independent

Options for Independent Work

- Independent Reading
- Word Study
- Vocabulary in Context Cards 181–188
- Listening Center: respond in Reader's Notebook
- Reader's Notebook: see writing prompt
- Ready-Made Work Stations, Lesson 26: Comprehension and Fluency, Word Study, Think and Write

See Teacher's Edition Lesson 26 for more independent activity options.

Writing About Reading

- Prompt: In *The Dot*, Vashti's teacher wants her to try something new. Draw or write about a time when you tried something new. What did you learn?
- Have children use their Reader's Notebook to record reactions to the literature they read and listened to this week.

GROUP SHARE Wrap up each day's Readers' Workshop by asking children to share how they applied the minilesson principle to their independent reading. Look for the Group Share section at the end of each minilesson.

Whole Group

Interactive Read-Aloud/ Shared Reading

- *What Can You Do?* by Shelly Rotner, Student Book: Lesson 27 INFORMATIONAL TEXT
- *The Shoemaker and the Elves,* Teacher's Edition: Lesson 27 FAIRY TALE
- *The Wind and the Sun,* Student Book: Lesson 27 FABLE

Whole-Group Links

You may use the suggested links to teach and reinforce skills in shared reading.

- *Base Words/Inflections* -er, -est; *change* y *to* i PHONICS
- *Syllable* -le PHONICS
- *Introduce Vocabulary (Vocabulary in Context Cards 189–196)* WORD STUDY
- *Classification/Categorization of Words: Emotions* VOCABULARY STRATEGIES

Reading Minilessons

- Text and Graphic Features: Words and Pictures, p. 92
- Genre: Fairy Tale, p. 93
- Genre: Fable, p. 93

Use the minilessons in this guide as a bridge between shared reading experiences and guided/ independent reading.

Small Group

Guided Reading

Select texts according to your children's instructional level. You may use the books below or select from the Leveled Readers Database, pp. 112–123. For instructional support, use the Leveled Readers Teacher's Guides along with the books that you choose.

- **LEVEL E**   *Helping at Home* (Vocabulary Reader) INFORMATIONAL TEXT
- **LEVEL E**   *Our Class* INFORMATIONAL TEXT
- **LEVEL H**   *A Fun Baseball Game* (Language Support) INFORMATIONAL TEXT
- **LEVEL I**   *The Baseball Game* INFORMATIONAL TEXT
- **LEVEL K**   *Always Learning* INFORMATIONAL TEXT

For strategic intervention, use the Write-In Reader: *What Can You Do?*

Small-Group Links

- *Text and Graphic Features; Analyze/ Evaluate* COMPREHENSION
- *Base Words/Inflections* -er, -est; *change* y *to* i PHONICS
- *Syllable* -le PHONICS
- *Intonation* FLUENCY
- *Classification/Categorization of Words: Emotions* VOCABULARY STRATEGIES

Literature Discussion

You may want to call together small groups for literature discussion. See pp. 124–128 for suggested trade book titles.

Independent

Options for Independent Work

- Independent Reading
- Word Study
- Vocabulary in Context Cards 189–196
- Listening Center: respond in Reader's Notebook
- Reader's Notebook: see writing prompt
- Ready-Made Work Stations, Lesson 27: Comprehension and Fluency, Word Study, Think and Write

See Teacher's Edition Lesson 27 for more independent activity options.

Writing About Reading

- Prompt: *The Wind and the Sun* is a story that teaches a lesson. Draw or write about another story that teaches a lesson.
- Have children use their Reader's Notebook to record reactions to the literature they read and listened to this week.

GROUP SHARE Wrap up each day's Readers' Workshop by asking children to share how they applied the minilesson principle to their independent reading. Look for the Group Share section at the end of each minilesson.

Suggested Weekly Focus

Lesson 28

Whole Group

Interactive Read-Aloud/ Shared Reading

- *The Kite* by Arnold Lobel, Student Book: Lesson 28 FANTASY
- *A Hopeful Song,* Teacher's Edition: Lesson 28 INFORMATIONAL TEXT
- *Measuring Weather,* Student Book: Lesson 28 INFORMATIONAL TEXT

Whole-Group Links

You may use the suggested links to teach and reinforce skills in shared reading.

- *Long* i *Spelling Patterns* igh, y, ie PHONICS
- *Base Words/Inflections* -ed, -ing, -er, -est, -es PHONICS
- *Introduce Vocabulary* (Vocabulary in Context Cards 197–204) WORD STUDY
- *Homographs* VOCABULARY STRATEGIES

Reading Minilessons

- Story Structure: How Characters Solve a Problem, p. 94
- Genre: Informational Text, p. 95
- Genre: Informational Text, p. 95

Use the minilessons in this guide as a bridge between shared reading experiences and guided/ independent reading.

Small Group

Guided Reading

Select texts according to your children's instructional level. You may use the books below or select from the Leveled Readers Database, pp. 112–123. For instructional support, use the Leveled Readers Teacher's Guides along with the books that you choose.

- **LEVEL F** *A Chunk of Cheese* FANTASY
- **LEVEL F** *Kite Flying* (Vocabulary Reader) INFORMATIONAL TEXT
- **LEVEL J** *The Boat Race* (Language Support) FANTASY
- **LEVEL J** *The Sailboat Race* FANTASY
- **LEVEL K** *The Sand Castle* FANTASY

For strategic intervention, use the Write-In Reader: *Mighty Little Mole.*

Small-Group Links

- *Story Structure; Infer/Predict* COMPREHENSION
- *Long* i *Spelling Patterns* igh, y, ie PHONICS
- *Base Words/Inflections* -ed, -ing, -er, -est, -es PHONICS
- *Phrasing: Natural Pauses* FLUENCY
- *Homographs* VOCABULARY STRATEGIES

Literature Discussion

You may want to call together small groups for literature discussion. See pp. 124–128 for suggested trade book titles.

Independent

Options for Independent Work

- Independent Reading
- Word Study
- Vocabulary in Context Cards 197–204
- Listening Center: respond in Reader's Notebook
- Reader's Notebook: see writing prompt
- Ready-Made Work Stations, Lesson 28: Comprehension and Fluency, Word Study, Think and Write

See Teacher's Edition Lesson 28 for more independent activity options.

Writing About Reading

- Prompt: In *The Kite,* Toad wants to quit and go home when the kite won't fly. Write a letter to Toad telling him why it is important not to give up.
- Have children use their Reader's Notebook to record reactions to the literature they read and listened to this week.

GROUP SHARE Wrap up each day's Readers' Workshop by asking children to share how they applied the minilesson principle to their independent reading. Look for the Group Share section at the end of each minilesson.

Whole Group

Interactive Read-Aloud/ Shared Reading

- *A Boat Disappears* by Doug Cushman, Student Book: Lesson 29 MYSTERY
- *A Stone Goes to Court*, Teacher's Edition: Lesson 29 FOLKTALE
- *Busy Bugs*, Student Book: Lesson 29 POETRY

Whole-Group Links

You may use the suggested links to teach and reinforce skills in shared reading.

- *Suffixes* -ful, -ly, -y PHONICS
- *Long Vowel Spelling Patterns:* a, e, i, o, u PHONICS
- *Introduce Vocabulary (Vocabulary in Context Cards 205–212)* WORD STUDY
- *Prefix* un- VOCABULARY STRATEGIES

Reading Minilessons

- Cause and Effect: Why Characters Do Something, p. 96
- Cause and Effect: Reasons Characters Do What They Do, p. 97
- Genre: Poetry, p. 97

Use the minilessons in this guide as a bridge between shared reading experiences and guided/ independent reading.

Small Group

Guided Reading

Select texts according to your children's instructional level. You may use the books below or select from the Leveled Readers Database, pp. 112–123. For instructional support, use the Leveled Readers Teacher's Guides along with the books that you choose.

- **LEVEL E** *Sink or Float?* (Vocabulary Reader) INFORMATIONAL TEXT
- **LEVEL F** *The Missing Glove* MYSTERY
- **LEVEL H** *Where Is Cow's Lunch?* (Language Support) MYSTERY
- **LEVEL I** *Cow's Lunch* MYSTERY
- **LEVEL K** *The Barnyard Bandit* MYSTERY

For strategic intervention, use the Write-In Reader: *Stick Bug's Awful Idea.*

Small-Group Links

- *Cause and Effect; Visualize* COMPREHENSION
- *Suffixes* -ful, -ly, -y PHONICS
- *Long Vowel Spelling Patterns:* a, e, i, o, u PHONICS
- *Expression* FLUENCY
- *Prefix* un- VOCABULARY STRATEGIES

Literature Discussion

You may want to call together small groups for literature discussion. See pp. 124–128 for suggested trade book titles.

Independent

Options for Independent Work

- Independent Reading
- Word Study
- Vocabulary in Context Cards 205–212
- Listening Center: respond in Reader's Notebook
- Reader's Notebook: see writing prompt
- Ready-Made Work Stations, Lesson 29: Comprehension and Fluency, Word Study, Think and Write

See Teacher's Edition Lesson 29 for more independent activity options.

Writing About Reading

- Prompt: *Busy Bugs* is a collection of poems about bugs. Write your own poem that would fit with the rest of these poems.
- Have children use their Reader's Notebook to record reactions to the literature they read and listened to this week.

GROUP SHARE Wrap up each day's Readers' Workshop by asking children to share how they applied the minilesson principle to their independent reading. Look for the Group Share section at the end of each minilesson.

Whole Group

Interactive Read-Aloud/ Shared Reading

- *Winners Never Quit!* by Mia Hamm, Student Book: Lesson 30 NARRATIVE NONFICTION
- *The Parts of the House Have a Fight,* Teacher's Edition: Lesson 30 FOLKTALE
- *Be a Team Player,* Student Book: Lesson 30 INFORMATIONAL TEXT

Whole-Group Links

You may use the suggested links to teach and reinforce skills in shared reading.

- *Syllabication (CV)* PHONICS
- *Prefixes un-, re-* PHONICS
- *Introduce Vocabulary (Vocabulary in Context Cards 213–220)* WORD STUDY
- *Suffix -ly* VOCABULARY STRATEGIES

Reading Minilessons

- Understanding Characters: What Characters Say and Do, p. 98
- Genre: Folktale, p. 99
- Genre: Informational Text, p. 99

Use the minilessons in this guide as a bridge between shared reading experiences and guided/ independent reading.

Small Group

Guided Reading

Select texts according to your children's instructional level. You may use the books below or select from the Leveled Readers Database, pp. 112–123. For instructional support, use the Leveled Readers Teacher's Guides along with the books that you choose.

- **LEVEL F** *Michelle Wie* NARRATIVE NONFICTION
- **LEVEL G** *Soccer* (Vocabulary Reader) INFORMATIONAL TEXT
- **LEVEL J** *Two Sisters Play Tennis* (Language Support) NARRATIVE NONFICTION
- **LEVEL J** *The Williams Sisters* NARRATIVE NONFICTION
- **LEVEL L** *Lance Armstrong* NARRATIVE NONFICTION

For strategic intervention, use the Write-In Reader: *Soccer Sisters.*

Small-Group Links

- *Understanding Characters; Summarize* COMPREHENSION
- *Syllabication (CV)* PHONICS
- *Prefixes un-, re-* PHONICS
- *Rate: Adjust Reading Rate to Purpose* FLUENCY
- *Suffix -ly* VOCABULARY STRATEGIES

Literature Discussion

You may want to call together small groups for literature discussion. See pp. 124–128 for suggested trade book titles.

Independent

Options for Independent Work

- Independent Reading
- Word Study
- Vocabulary in Context Cards 213–220
- Listening Center: respond in Reader's Notebook
- Reader's Notebook: see writing prompt
- Ready-Made Work Stations, Lesson 30: Comprehension and Fluency, Word Study, Think and Write

See Teacher's Edition Lesson 30 for more independent activity options.

Writing About Reading

- Prompt: *Winners Never Quit!* tells Mia's story about playing soccer. Draw or write about the most important things that happen in the beginning, middle, and end of the story.
- Have children use their Reader's Notebook to record reactions to the literature they read and listened to this week.

GROUP SHARE Wrap up each day's Readers' Workshop by asking children to share how they applied the minilesson principle to their independent reading. Look for the Group Share section at the end of each minilesson.

Whole-Group Lessons

Whole-group lessons provide a context for all children to think about what they read, learn from their peers' ideas, and demonstrate understanding of specific skills. To prepare for each lesson sequence on the pages that follow, we suggest that you:

- Read the literature in advance, and use self-stick notes to mark the suggested stopping points. As needed, supplement with questions that address your students' needs and allow for spontaneity of your students' responses.

- Set up an easel with chart paper (or use an overhead projector or whiteboard) to display minilesson principles and to share graphic organizers that you will complete with children.

Lesson 1...40

Lesson 2...42

Lesson 3...44

Lesson 4...46

Lesson 5...48

Lesson 6...50

Lesson 7...52

Lesson 8...54

Lesson 9...56

Lesson 10...58

Lesson 11...60

Lesson 12...62

Lesson 13...64

Lesson 14...66

Lesson 15...68

Lesson 16...70

Lesson 17...72

Lesson 18...74

Lesson 19...76

Lesson 20...78

Lesson 21...80

Lesson 22...82

Lesson 23...84

Lesson 24...86

Lesson 25...88

Lesson 26...90

Lesson 27...92

Lesson 28...94

Lesson 29...96

Lesson 30...98

Whole-Group Lessons

What Is a Pal?
Student Book, Lesson 1

The Lion and the Mouse
Teacher's Edition, Lesson 1

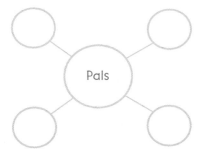

Friends Forever
Student Book, Lesson 1

▶ **What Is a Pal?**

INTERACTIVE READ-ALOUD/SHARED READING

Read the book aloud to children. Stop periodically for very brief discussion of the book. Use the following suggested stopping points and prompts for quick group response, or give a specific prompt and have partners or threes turn and talk.

- After children read that Sam and Nat can help Dan, ask: "How are these pals helping? How do you know that?"
- After children read about who can be a pal, ask: "Who can be a pal? Who are some of your pals? Turn and talk about your ideas with a partner."
- After children read that a pal is fun to be with, ask: "What do you do with your pals?" Follow-up: "Why are your pals fun to be with?"
- At the end, ask: "How are you a pal?"

MINILESSON Main Idea

TEACH Display the minilesson principle on chart paper, and read it aloud to children. Tell children they are going to learn how to notice that authors tell mostly about one thing in information books.

1. Discuss the principle with children, using *What Is a Pal?* as an example. Suggested language: "There are different kinds of books. Some books tell stories. Other books give information or tell about real things. What kind of book is *What Is a Pal?*" *(an information book)* Follow-up: "How do you know?" *(It gives information about pals.)*

> **MINILESSON PRINCIPLE**
>
> Notice that authors tell mostly about one thing in information books.

2. Focus on one part of the book, such as what pals can do with you. Suggested language: "This book tells about some things a pal can do with you. What are two things a pal can do with you?" *(A pal can help you and play with you.)*

3. Use children's responses to explain that authors tell mostly about one thing in information books. Suggested language: "The author tells mostly about pals. Pals are the one thing that this information book is mostly about."

4. Elicit from children additional details that support the idea that pals are the one thing this book is mostly about. Record children's ideas in a Web like the one shown here.

```
        ( )        ( )
          \       /
           \     /
          ( Pals )
           /     \
          /       \
        ( )        ( )
```

SUMMARIZE AND APPLY Restate the minilesson principle. Then tell children to apply it to their independent reading. Suggested language: "When you read an information book, think about the one thing that the author tells mostly about. Think about how you know what that one thing is."

GROUP SHARE Ask children to share what they learned from reading an information book. Tell children to identify the one thing that the author tells mostly about and how they identified it.

▶ The Lion and the Mouse

INTERACTIVE READ-ALOUD/SHARED READING

Read aloud the story to children. Stop periodically for brief discussion of the story. Use the following suggested stopping points and prompts:

- After the lion releases the mouse, ask: "Why does the lion let the mouse go?"
- After the mouse runs to find the lion, ask: "Why do you think the mouse comes back to help the lion?"
- At the end of the story, say: "How did the lion feel at the end of the story? Turn and talk about your ideas with a partner."

MINILESSON Genre: Fable

TEACH Display the minilesson principle on chart paper, and read it aloud to children. Explain that *The Lion and the Mouse* is a fable and that a fable is a story that has a lesson. Tell children they are going to think about how the lion in this fable learns a lesson.

1. Discuss with children the character of the lion. Suggested language: "What was the lion like at the beginning of the story?" *(He thought he was better than anyone else because he was the King of Beasts.)*

> **MINILESSON PRINCIPLE**
>
> Think about how the people or animals in a story learn a lesson.

2. Talk with children about how the lion changed by the end of the story. Suggested language: "What was the lion like at the end of the story? What lesson did he learn?" *(He found out that he wasn't as powerful as he had thought. He learned that as powerful as he was, he needed help from a small, unimportant mouse.)*

3. Discuss with children the lessons that people or animals have learned in other stories they have read before. Write their ideas in a T-Map labeled *People or Animals* and *Lesson Learned*.

SUMMARIZE AND APPLY Restate the minilesson principle. Tell children to apply it to their independent reading. Suggested language: "When you read, think about how the people or animals in a story learn a lesson."

GROUP SHARE Ask children to share an example from independent reading of how the people or animals in a story learn a lesson.

▶ Friends Forever

INTERACTIVE READ-ALOUD/SHARED READING

Read aloud the introduction and the poems to children. Stop periodically for brief discussion. Use the following suggested stopping points and prompts:

- After reading "Damon & Blue," ask: "What is this poem about?" Follow-up: "What does the poet mean when she says *Can't beat us when we're side by side*?"
- After reading "Wait for Me," ask: "What is this poem about?" Follow-up: "How is this poem like 'Damon & Blue'? Turn and talk about your ideas with a partner."

MINILESSON Genre: Poetry

TEACH Remind children that they have read three poems: "Damon & Blue," "Wait for Me," and "Jambo." Explain to children that some poems have words that rhyme, which can make them fun to read.

1. Model how to notice rhyming words in poems. Read aloud the first three lines of "Damon & Blue," emphasizing the word at the end of each line. Have children follow along. Then say the three rhyming words in isolation: *Blue, two, avenue.* Point out that these words rhyme because they have the same ending sound.

> **MINILESSON PRINCIPLE**
>
> Notice that some poems have words that rhyme.

2. Help children notice the rhyming words in poems. Read aloud the remaining lines of "Damon & Blue," and help children identify the rhyming words *glide, stride*, and *side*. Repeat with "Wait for Me" and "Jambo."

3. Ask children to share what they noticed about the poems they read, prompting them to recognize that some poems have words that rhyme. Then write the minilesson principle on chart paper, and read it aloud. Explain to children that noticing rhyming words in a poem will help them enjoy it more.

SUMMARIZE AND APPLY Restate the minilesson principle. Tell children to apply it to their independent reading. Suggested language: "When you read poems, notice that some of them have words that rhyme."

GROUP SHARE Ask children to tell about poems with rhyming words that they read for independent reading. Have them explain how the rhyming words made the poems fun to read.

Whole-Group Lessons

The Storm
Student Book, Lesson 2

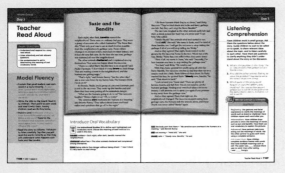

Susie and the Bandits
Teacher's Edition, Lesson 2

Storms!
Student Book, Lesson 2

▶ **The Storm**

INTERACTIVE READ-ALOUD/SHARED READING

Read aloud the story to children. Stop periodically for very brief discussion of the story. Use the following suggested stopping points and prompts for quick group response, or give a specific prompt and have partners or threes turn and talk.

- After Tim and Rip run to Pop, ask: "Who are the people and animals in this story? Where does the story take place?"
- After Pop tells Tim to go to bed, ask: "Why is Pop at Tim's house? How do you know? Turn and talk about your ideas with a partner."
- After Rip hides, ask: "Why do Tim and Rip hide?" Follow-up: "What do you think will happen next?"
- At the end of the story, ask: "What does Pop do for Tim? How does this help Tim?"

MINILESSON Understanding Characters

TEACH Display the minilesson principle on chart paper, and read it aloud to children. Tell children they are going to learn how to think about the people and animals in a story to understand how they feel.

1. Discuss the principle with children, using examples of characters from *The Storm.* Suggested language: "In the story *The Storm,* we got to know a few people and animals as we read. Who were these people and animals?" *(Pop, Tim, and Rip)*

> **MINILESSON PRINCIPLE**
>
> Notice what the people and animals do to help you understand how they feel.

2. Focus on Tim and Rip in the story. Suggested language: "What did Tim and Rip see out the window when they went to bed?" *(Tim and Rip saw a lightning storm.)* Follow-up: "What did they do?" *(They hid.)*

3. Use children's responses to explain that what people and animals do in a story are clues that help readers understand how the people and animals feel. Suggested language: "The author uses what Tim and Rip did (hid) to show readers that Tim and Rip were afraid of the lightning storm."

4. Elicit from children additional examples from the story. Record children's ideas in a T-Map like the one shown here.

What the Person or Animal Did	How the Person or Animal Felt

SUMMARIZE AND APPLY Restate the minilesson principle. Then tell children to apply it to their independent reading. Suggested language: "When you read, think about what the people and animals do in stories. Find out about how they feel by noticing what they do."

GROUP SHARE Ask children to share what they learned about one person or animal in their story. Tell them to explain what the person or animal did that helped them learn about how the person or animal felt.

▶ Susie and the Bandits

INTERACTIVE READ-ALOUD/SHARED READING

Read aloud the story to children. Stop periodically for brief discussion of it. Use the following suggested stopping points and prompts:

- After Paulie Opossum speaks, ask: "What is the problem in this story?"
- After the raccoons run to the creek for a bath, ask: "How did Susie Skunk get the bandits to stop? What do you think will happen next?"
- At the end of the story, say: "Susie Skunk tells the raccoons that finding their own food takes a lot more bravery. What do you think she meant? Turn and talk about your ideas with a partner."

MINILESSON Understanding Characters

TEACH Display the minilesson principle on chart paper, and read it aloud to children. Tell children they are going to learn to think about what characters, the people and animals in a story, do to understand what they are like.

1. Using the character Susie from *Susie and the Bandits,* discuss with children that the way characters act gives clues about what they are like. Suggested language: "In the story *Susie and the Bandits,* Susie made a deal with the other animals. What was the deal she made?" *(Susie promised to get the raccoons to stop raiding the garbage if the animals would stop calling her Stinky.)*

> **MINILESSON PRINCIPLE**
>
> Think about what characters do to understand what they are like.

2. Talk with children about Susie's reason for making that deal. Suggested language: "Susie wanted the animals to stop calling her Stinky. Why did Susie want that?" *(Being called Stinky hurt her feelings.)* Follow-up: "What did her plan show about her?" *(She was smart because she thought of a way to make everyone happy.)*

3. Discuss with children the raccoons' actions in the story and how those actions showed what the characters were like. Write their ideas in a T-Map labeled *What the Character Did* and *What the Character Was Like.*

SUMMARIZE AND APPLY Restate the minilesson principle. Tell children to apply it to their independent reading. Suggested language: "When you read, think about what characters do to help you understand what the characters are like."

GROUP SHARE Ask children to share an example from independent reading of something a character does and how it shows what the character is like.

▶ Storms!

INTERACTIVE READ-ALOUD/SHARED READING

Read aloud the book to children. Stop periodically for brief discussion. Use the following suggested stopping points and prompts:

- After the section about kinds of storms, ask: "What is this book mostly about?" Follow-up: "What are some kinds of storms?"
- At the end of the book, ask: "What are some tools for measuring storms?" Follow-up: "Why is it important for scientists to measure storms? Turn and talk about your ideas with a partner."

MINILESSON Genre: Informational Text

TEACH Tell children they are going to think about the information the author tells in *Storms!*

1. Discuss the principle with children, using *Storms!* as an example. Suggested language: "There are different kinds of books. Some books tell stories. Other books give information or tell about facts. What kind of book is *Storms!*?" *(an information book)* Follow-up: "How do you know?" *(It gives information and facts about storms.)*

> **MINILESSON PRINCIPLE**
>
> Think about the information the author tells.

2. Ask children to share the information from *Storms!* Suggested language: "What information do you remember from *Storms!*?" *(Answers will vary.)* Follow-up: "What information did you think was most interesting? Why?" *(Answers will vary.)* Then guide children to retell facts from *Storms!* as you write the minilesson principle on chart paper. Explain to children that thinking about the information the author tells will help them understand what they read in an information book.

SUMMARIZE AND APPLY Restate the minilesson principle. Tell children to apply it to their independent reading. Suggested language: "When you read an information book, think about the information the author tells."

GROUP SHARE Ask children to share some information from an information book that they read for independent reading.

Whole-Group Lessons

▶ Curious George at School

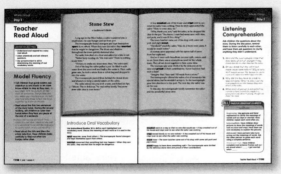

Curious George at School
Student Book, Lesson 3

Stone Stew
Teacher's Edition, Lesson 3

School Long Ago
Student Book, Lesson 3

INTERACTIVE READ-ALOUD/SHARED READING

Read aloud the story to children. Stop periodically for very brief discussion of the story. Use the following suggested stopping points and prompts for quick group response, or give a specific prompt and have partners or threes turn and talk.

- After George can see the paints, ask: "Who is the most important character in this story? Where is he?"
- After George spills the paints, ask: "What problem does George have? How do you think he will solve his problem? Turn and talk about your ideas with a partner."
- After George gets a mop, ask: "How is George going to try to solve his problem? How do you know?" Follow up: "What do you think will happen next?"
- At the end of the story, ask: "What happened when George tried to clean up the mess by himself? How did the mess get cleaned up?"

MINILESSON Sequence of Events

TEACH Display the minilesson principle on chart paper, and read it aloud to children. Tell children they are going to think about what happens first, next, and last in a story. Explain that thinking about the story events in order will help them better understand the story.

1. Use *Curious George at School* to discuss the principle with children. Suggested language: "What happened in the beginning of the story *Curious George at School*?" (*A monkey named Curious George went to school.*) Follow-up: "What problem did George have first?" (*He made a mess with the paints.*)

> **MINILESSON PRINCIPLE**
>
> Think about what happens first, next, and last in the story.

2. Tell children to think about how George tried to solve his problem after he made a mess. Suggested language: "First George made a mess with the paints. What happened next?" (*He tried to clean up the paints and made an even bigger mess.*)

3. Ask children to think about how the story ended. Suggested language: "First George made a mess with the paints. Next he tried to clean up the paints and made an even bigger mess. What happened last, at the end of the story?" (*The children helped George clean up the mess.*)

4. Work with children to use their answers to the previous questions to tell what happened first, next, and last in the story. Point out that using the words *first, next,* and *last* will help them remember the order of what happened. Record children's ideas in a Flow Chart like the one shown here.

> First
> ↓
> Next
> ↓
> Last

SUMMARIZE AND APPLY Restate the minilesson principle. Explain to children that they can apply it to their independent reading. Suggested language: "When you read a story, think about what happens first, next, and last."

GROUP SHARE Have children share stories they read by telling what happened first, next, and last. Remind them to use the words *first, next,* and *last* to help tell the correct order of what happened.

▶ Stone Stew

INTERACTIVE READ-ALOUD/SHARED READING

Read aloud the story to children. Stop periodically for brief discussion of the story. Use the following suggested stopping points and prompts:

- After the sailor asks for a bite to eat, ask: "What did the townspeople do when the sailor came into town? Why?"
- After the boy gives the sailor some okra, ask: "Why does the boy have to sneak to give the sailor okra?"
- At the end of the story, say: "Think about the townspeople. What kind of people are they?" Follow-up: "Think about the sailor. What kind of person is he? Turn and talk about your ideas with a partner."

MINILESSON Sequence of Events

TEACH Display the minilesson principle on chart paper, and read it aloud to children. Remind children that thinking about what happens first, next, and last in a story will help them better understand what the story is about.

1. Help children identify the sequence of events in *Stone Stew*. Suggested language: "In *Stone Stew*, what happened first when the sailor comes to town?" *(He asked for food, but the townspeople wouldn't give him any.)*

> **MINILESSON PRINCIPLE**
>
> Think about what happens first, next, and last in the story.

2. Tell children to think about what the sailor did next to solve this problem. Suggested language: "First the sailor asked for food, but the townspeople wouldn't give him any. So what did the sailor do next?" *(He took out a stone and began to make stone stew.)*

3. Ask children to think about how the problem was solved at the end of the story. Suggested language: "First the sailor asked for food, but the townspeople wouldn't give him any. So, next, he took out a stone and began to make stone stew. What happened last?" *(One at a time the townspeople added foods to the stew, and they all ate the stew with the sailor.)*

4. Work with children to use their answers to the previous questions to tell what happened first, next, and last in the story. Write their ideas in a Flow Chart labeled *First, Next,* and *Last.*

SUMMARIZE AND APPLY Restate the minilesson principle. Explain to children that they should apply it to their independent reading. Suggested language: "When you read a story, think about what happens first, next, and last. This will help you understand what the story is about."

GROUP SHARE Have children tell what happened first, next, and last in a story they read.

▶ School Long Ago

INTERACTIVE READ-ALOUD/SHARED READING

Read aloud the book to children. Stop periodically for brief discussion. Use the following suggested stopping points and prompts:

- After the first paragraph, ask: "What will this book be mostly about? How do you know?"
- At the end, ask: "What are some of the ways school was different long ago? Turn and talk about your ideas with a partner."

MINILESSON Genre: Informational Text

TEACH Explain to children that *School Long Ago* is different from the other two stories they read this week. Point out that the book gives information about real people, places, and things that happened. Display the minilesson principle on chart paper, and read it aloud to children. Explain that an information book may include charts that give information.

1. Help children understand the information in the chart. Suggested language: "What are the words at the top of the columns?" *(Then, Now)* "Why is the slate in the *Then* column and the notebook in the *Now* column?" *(They show what children wrote on in school long ago and what they use today.)* Follow-up: "Why are the slate and the notebook next to each other in this chart?" *(They are both writing tools. The chart shows them next to each other to tell about how tools have changed.)*

> **MINILESSON PRINCIPLE**
>
> Notice how the charts in a book give information.

2. Discuss how charts give information. Suggested language: "This chart uses words and pictures to give information. What information does this chart help you understand?" *(how school has changed from long ago)* Help children understand that authors use charts to show information in a way that is easy to understand. Explain that reading charts for information will help them better understand what they read.

SUMMARIZE AND APPLY Restate the minilesson principle. Tell children to apply it to their independent reading. Suggested language: "When you read, look for charts and read them to understand the information they give."

GROUP SHARE Ask children to share examples of charts in the books they chose for independent reading and tell about the information the charts give.

Whole-Group Lessons

Lucia's Neighborhood
Student Book, Lesson 4

Painting Word Pictures
Teacher's Edition, Lesson 4

City Mouse and Country Mouse
Student Book, Lesson 4

▶ Lucia's Neighborhood

INTERACTIVE READ-ALOUD/SHARED READING

Read aloud the book to children. Stop periodically for very brief discussion of it. Use the following suggested stopping points and prompts for quick group response, or give a specific prompt and have partners or threes turn and talk.

- After Lucia visits the pet shop, ask: "Is there a pattern in this book? What is it?"
- After Lucia and her mother stop in the street, ask: "How is Lucia's neighborhood like your neighborhood? How is it different?"
- After Lucia visits the library, ask: "Which place in Lucia's neighborhood would you most like to visit? Why? Turn and talk about your ideas with a partner."
- At the end of the story, ask: "Why do you think Lucia says that it's fun to be home?" Follow-up: "How do you feel when you get home after a busy day?"

MINILESSON Text and Graphic Features

TEACH Display the minilesson principle on chart paper, and read it aloud to children.

1. Guide children through the process of using pictures to understand the words in *Lucia's Neighborhood*. Display the page that shows the bakery. Cover the text and ask: "What do you see in this picture?" *(Lucia is eating a pastry. One woman has a tray of pastries. Another woman wears a white apron. Behind the people are display cases with rolls and muffins.)*

   > **MINILESSON PRINCIPLE**
   >
   > You can look at the pictures to understand the words.

2. Tell children to think about all the clues in the picture. Then point to the word at the top of the page and ask: "How could you use the picture clues to figure out the word at the top of the picture?" *(You could tell from the picture that they are at a bakery. The word at the top of the page begins with* b, *so I can guess that is says* bakery.*)*

3. Ask children to reread the sentences at the bottom of this page. Then talk about how the clues from the picture help them better understand the words. Suggested language: "What is Lucia talking about when she says *Look what we get here*?" *(They get pastries to eat.)* Follow-up: "How do you know?" *(You can tell by looking at the picture.)*

4. Work with children to explain how to use clues in other pictures to better understand the words in this book. Record children's ideas in a T-Map like the one shown here.

What the Pictures Show	What the Words Say

SUMMARIZE AND APPLY Restate the minilesson principle. Explain to children that they can apply it to their independent reading. Suggested language: "When you read a book, look at the pictures to help you read words you don't know and to understand what is happening."

GROUP SHARE Have children share books they read and explain how they used pictures to figure out a word or understand what they read.

▶ Painting Word Pictures

INTERACTIVE READ-ALOUD/SHARED READING

Read aloud the introduction and the poems to children. Stop periodically for brief discussion. Use the following suggested stopping points and prompts:

- After the introduction, ask: "How are poets like painters?"
- After "The Wind," ask: "Which words rhyme in this poem?" Follow-up: "How do they make the poem more fun to read?"
- After "Autumn Leaves," ask: "How is this poem like a song? Turn and talk about your ideas with a partner."

MINILESSON Genre: Poetry

TEACH Display the minilesson principle on chart paper, and read it aloud to children. Tell children they are going to think about how poems make pictures in their minds.

1. Ask children to close their eyes and listen as you reread the first two lines of "The Wind." Then have them describe the word picture it created. Suggested language: "What did you see in your mind when I read these lines?" *(the wind blowing kites and birds around the sky)*

> **MINILESSON PRINCIPLE**
>
> Think about how words in poems make pictures in your mind.

2. Ask children to close their eyes and listen as you reread the last stanza of "Autumn Leaves." Next ask volunteers to pretend they are autumn leaves and act out what they do when they are tired, as others watch. Then ask children to think about the picture they made in their own minds when they heard these words. Suggested language: "How was the picture in your mind like what the children acted out? How was it different?"

3. Discuss with children other word pictures in "The Wind" and "Autumn Leaves." Write their ideas in a T-Map labeled *Words in the Poem* and *Pictures in My Mind.*

SUMMARIZE AND APPLY Restate the minilesson principle. Explain to children that they should apply it to their independent reading. Suggested language: "When you read a poem, think about how the words make pictures in your mind. This will help you understand and enjoy the poem."

GROUP SHARE After reading a poem, have children describe or draw the picture the poem made in their mind.

▶ City Mouse and Country Mouse

INTERACTIVE READ-ALOUD/SHARED READING

Before reading, discuss the format of this play with children. Then read it aloud, using different voices for the characters or ask three volunteers to take the parts and read them aloud. Stop periodically for brief discussion of the play. Use the following suggested stopping points and prompts:

- After the second page, ask: "Why didn't City Mouse want to go to the country? How do you know?"
- At the end of the story, ask: "How is the city different from the country? Turn and talk about your ideas with a partner."

MINILESSON Genre: Fable

TEACH Display the minilesson principle on chart paper, and read it aloud to children. Explain that *City Mouse and Country Mouse* is a fable and that a fable is a story that has a lesson. Tell children they are going to think about how a character in this fable learned a lesson.

1. Discuss the character Country Mouse and why he went to the city. Suggested language: "Why did Country Mouse go to the city?" *(City Mouse wouldn't visit him in the country and said the food was better in the city.)*

> **MINILESSON PRINCIPLE**
>
> Think about the lesson that a character learns in a story.

2. Talk about what Country Mouse thought about the city at first and why this changed. Suggested language: "What did Country Mouse think about the city at first?" *(He liked it.)* "How do you know?" *(He said,* Look at all this yummy food!*)* Follow-up: "What made Country Mouse change his mind?" *(A cat tried to eat him and City Mouse.)*

3. Discuss the lesson in this story. Suggested language: "Why did Country Mouse go back to the country?" *(He wanted to be safe.)* Follow-up: "What lesson did he learn?" *(It is better to live in a safe place than in one that has nicer things but is very dangerous.)*

4. Discuss with children the lessons that characters have learned in other stories they have read before. Write their ideas in a T-Map labeled *Character* and *Lesson Learned.*

SUMMARIZE AND APPLY Restate the minilesson principle. Tell children to apply it to their independent reading. Suggested language: "When you read, think about the lesson a character learns."

GROUP SHARE Ask children to share an example from independent reading of a lesson that a character has learned.

Whole-Group Lessons

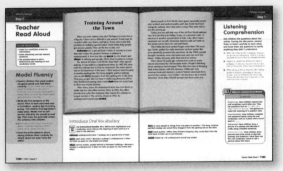

Gus Takes the Train
Student Book, Lesson 5

Training Around the Town
Teacher's Edition, Lesson 5

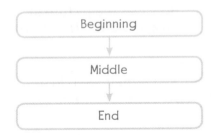

City Zoo
Student Book, Lesson 5

▶ Gus Takes the Train

INTERACTIVE READ-ALOUD/SHARED READING

Read aloud the story to children. Stop periodically for very brief discussion of the story. Use the following suggested stopping points and prompts for quick group response, or give a specific prompt and have partners or threes turn and talk.

- After the train conductor looks at his watch, ask: "Who is the most important character in this story? What is his problem?"
- After Gus sits, ask: "How does the train conductor help Gus?"
- After Peg and Gus have a sip, ask: "How do you think Gus feels about meeting a friend? How can you tell? Talk about your ideas with a partner."
- At the end of the story, ask: "What do you think Gus will do now that he is off the train?" Follow-up: "Why do you think so?"

MINILESSON Story Structure

TEACH Display the minilesson principle on chart paper, and read it aloud to children. Tell children that they are going to think about how a story begins and how it ends.

1. Discuss the principle with children, using *Gus Takes the Train*. Suggested language: "What happened in the beginning of the story *Gus Takes the Train*?" (*Gus ran to catch a train with a bag that was big and heavy.*) "How do you think he felt?" (*He probably felt worried that he would miss the train.*)

> **MINILESSON PRINCIPLE**
>
> Think about how a story begins and how it ends.

2. Tell children to think about what happened to Gus on the train and how the story ends. Suggested language: "What happened at the end of the story?" (*Gus and Peg got off the train at the zoo.*) "How did Gus feel then?" (*happy*) "Why was he happy?" (*He had fun on the train with Peg and may go to the zoo with her.*)

3. Work with children to use their answers to the previous questions to tell what happened in the beginning, middle, and end of the story. Record children's ideas in a Flow Chart like the one shown here.

> Beginning
>
> ↓
>
> Middle
>
> ↓
>
> End

SUMMARIZE AND APPLY Restate the minilesson principle. Explain to children that they can apply it to their independent reading. Suggested language: "When you read a story, think about how it begins and how it ends."

GROUP SHARE Have children each share a story they have read by telling how the story begins and how it ends. Suggest that they use the words *In the beginning* and *at the end of the story*.

▶ Training Around the Town

INTERACTIVE READ-ALOUD/SHARED READING

Read aloud the passage to children. Stop periodically for brief discussion. Use the following suggested stopping points and prompts:

- After reading the first paragraph, ask: "What problem do cities have?" Follow-up: "What is one way some cities solve this problem?"
- After reading about the closing of the Fort Worth subway, ask: "How was the Fort Worth subway special?"
- At the end of the passage, ask: "How are subways and streetcars the same? How are they different? Turn and talk about your ideas with a partner."

MINILESSON Genre: Informational Text

TEACH Display the minilesson principle on chart paper, and read it aloud to children. Tell children they are going to think about ideas that go together when they read.

1. Point out that *Training Around the Town* tells about two different kinds of city trains. Suggested language: "What two kinds of trains did you learn about?" *(subway and streetcar)*

   > **MINILESSON PRINCIPLE**
   >
   > Think about ideas that go together when you read.

2. Help children recall that the author first explained what a subway is and then told more about subways by describing a subway in Fort Worth. Explain that both of these ideas go together to help readers learn about subways.

3. Help children see the same pattern in the section about streetcars. Suggested language: "First the author explained what a streetcar is. What did the author describe next?" *(the Dallas streetcar system)* Follow-up: "Why did the author do that?" *(to help readers understand more about streetcars)*

4. Work with children to use their answers to the previous questions to complete an Idea-Support Map for the topic of streetcars.

SUMMARIZE AND APPLY Restate the minilesson principle. Explain to children that they should apply it to their independent reading. Suggested language: "When you read an information book, think about the ideas that go together. This will help you better understand what the book is about."

GROUP SHARE Have children tell about an information book that they read for independent reading by telling what it was about and the ideas that went together.

▶ City Zoo

INTERACTIVE READ-ALOUD/SHARED READING

Read aloud the book to children. Stop periodically for brief discussion. Use the following suggested stopping points and prompts:

- After reading the first page, ask: "What animals might you see at this zoo?" Follow-up: "Why do you think the author says the animals are interesting?"
- At the end of the book, ask: "Why does the author give these tips?" Follow-up: "How could they help if you went to a zoo? Turn and talk about your ideas with a partner."

MINILESSON Genre: Informational Text

TEACH Display the minilesson principle on chart paper, and read it aloud to children. Point out that *City Zoo* has a map and that maps use pictures and words to show where things are.

1. Help children understand the information in the map. Suggested language: "A map is a picture of a place. A key shows what the pictures on a map mean."

   > **MINILESSON PRINCIPLE**
   >
   > Notice how pictures and words go together in books.

2. Have children use the key to find and name different zoo animals on the map. Ask volunteers to demonstrate how they match the words on the key to the animal pictures on the map. Tell children that using these words and pictures together helps them learn where the animals are at the zoo. Explain that noticing how pictures and words go together will help them better understand books that have picture tools such as maps.

SUMMARIZE AND APPLY Restate the minilesson principle. Tell children to apply it to their independent reading. Suggested language: "When you read today, notice how pictures and words go together."

GROUP SHARE Ask children to share examples of maps and picture tools in the books they chose for independent reading. Have them tell about how the pictures and words go together.

Whole-Group Lessons

Jack and the Wolf
Student Book, Lesson 6

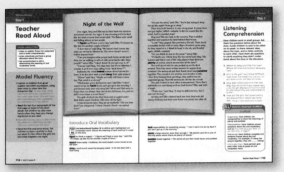

Night of the Wolf
Teacher's Edition, Lesson 6

The Three Little Pigs
Student Book, Lesson 6

▶ Jack and the Wolf

INTERACTIVE READ-ALOUD/SHARED READING

Read aloud the story to children. Stop periodically for very brief discussion of the story. Use the following suggested stopping points and prompts for quick group response, or give a specific prompt and have partners or threes turn and talk.

- After you read about Jack's job, ask: "Would you like to have Jack's job? Why or why not?"
- After Jack yells *Wolf!* the second time, ask: "What would you say to Jack if you were one of his friends? Tell why."
- After Jack says *You did not come,* ask: "Why didn't Jack's friends come when he called? Turn and talk about your ideas with a partner."
- At the end of the story, ask: "What lesson did Jack learn in this story?" Follow-up: "Is this a good lesson for other people to learn, too? Why?"

MINILESSON Understanding Characters

TEACH Display the minilesson principle on chart paper, and read it aloud to children. Tell children they are going to learn how to think about characters as they read. Point out that this will help them understand ways that characters change.

1. Discuss the principle with children, using examples of characters from *Jack and the Wolf.* Suggested language: "In the story *Jack and the Wolf,* you got to know a few different characters as you read. Who were they?" (*Jack, Jack's friends, Wolf, Nell*)

2. Focus on Jack and have children tell what he was like at the beginning of the story. Suggested language: "What did you learn about Jack at the beginning of the story?" (*Jack was a little boy. He sat with the sheep on a hill. He called* Wolf *over and over because he was bored.*)

3. Have children tell what Jack was like at the end of the story. Suggested language: "How did Jack feel when he promised Nell not to play tricks anymore? Do you think he will yell *Wolf* again just for fun?" (*Possible answer: Jack felt sorry that he had played a mean trick, so I don't think he will do it again.*)

4. Use children's responses to the above questions to fill in a T-Map labeled *Beginning* and *End* like the one shown here.

> **MINILESSON PRINCIPLE**
>
> Think about how the characters change.

Beginning	End

SUMMARIZE AND APPLY Restate the minilesson principle. Then tell children to apply it to their independent reading. Suggested language: "When you read, think about how the characters change in a story."

GROUP SHARE Ask children to share a description of a character they read about in a story. Tell them to explain how the character changed by the end of the story.

▶ Night of the Wolf

INTERACTIVE READ-ALOUD/SHARED READING

Read aloud the story to children. Stop periodically for brief discussion of the story. Use the following suggested stopping points and prompts:

- After the wind tosses a snow shovel across the yard, ask: "Where and when does this story take place?"
- After the girls hear the wolf howl a second time, ask: "What do you think will happen next? Turn and talk about your ideas with a partner."
- At the end of the story, say: "What happened right before Meg and Ellie saw the wolves run away? What happened after?"

MINILESSON Understanding Characters

TEACH Display the minilesson principle on chart paper, and read it aloud to children. Tell children they are going to learn to use what characters say and do to notice when characters are like real people.

1. Discuss with children how some story characters are like real people and others are not. Suggested language: "Think of a story character you know who could not be a real person." Discuss the characteristics that children used to figure it out. Ask: "What makes you think that character could not be real?"

> **MINILESSON PRINCIPLE**
>
> Notice when the characters in stories are like real people.

2. Guide children to think about Meg and Ellie in *Night of the Wolf*. Suggested language: "Think about what Meg and Ellie said and did. Were they like real people? What makes you think so?" *(Yes, they talked like real people and had feelings like real people. They wished they could have a snow day and were scared of the wolf's howl. These are both things real children might do.)*

SUMMARIZE AND APPLY Restate the minilesson principle. Tell children to apply it to their independent reading. Suggested language: "When you read, think about whether the characters are like real people and how you know."

GROUP SHARE Have children choose a character from a story they read and tell how they knew that the character was or was not like a real person.

▶ The Three Little Pigs

INTERACTIVE READ-ALOUD/SHARED READING

Read aloud the story to children. Stop periodically for brief discussion of the story. Use the following suggested stopping points and prompts:

- After the Wolf blows over the first house, ask: "Who are the important characters in the story so far? What are they like?"
- At the end of the story, ask: "What happened first in this story? What happened next? What happened last?"

MINILESSON Genre: Fairy Tale

TEACH Display the minilesson principle on chart paper, and read it aloud to children. Explain that *The Three Little Pigs* is different from the other two stories they read this week. Tell children that *The Three Little Pigs* is a special type of story called a fairy tale. Explain that they will think about whether the things that happen in a fairy tale could happen in real life.

1. Focus on *The Three Little Pigs* to introduce the idea that fairy tales tell about things that could not happen in real life. Suggested language: "The story *The Three Little Pigs* tells about things that could not happen in real life. In real life, a pig could not a build a house out of straw, sticks, or bricks."

> **MINILESSON PRINCIPLE**
>
> Think about what happens in a story and if it could really happen.

2. Ask children to name other things that happen in *The Three Little Pigs* that could not happen in real life. Guide children to explain how they know which events could happen in real life and which could not. Explain to children that they will better understand what they read if they pay attention to whether things that happen in a story could happen in real life.

SUMMARIZE AND APPLY Restate the minilesson principle. Tell children to apply it to their independent reading. Suggested language: "When you read, ask yourself whether what is happening in a story could happen in real life."

GROUP SHARE Ask children to tell something that happened in the story they read for independent reading and whether it could happen in real life.

Whole-Group Lessons

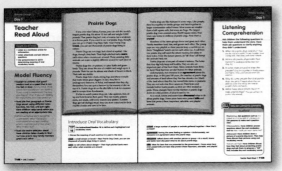

How Animals Communicate
Student Book, Lesson 7

Prairie Dogs
Teacher's Edition, Lesson 7

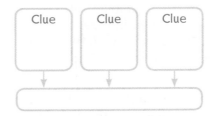

Insect Messages
Student Book, Lesson 7

▶ How Animals Communicate

INTERACTIVE READ-ALOUD/SHARED READING

Read aloud the book to children. Stop periodically for very brief discussion. Use the following suggested stopping points and prompts for quick group response, or give a specific prompt and have partners or threes turn and talk.

- After you read the section about how animals touch, ask: "What was this part about? What did you learn about animals?"
- Before you reach the page that shows a snake, pause to point out the heading. Read it aloud and ask: "What do you think this page will be about?"
- After you read the page that shows a skunk, ask: "How do the words and picture tell you that the skunk smells bad?"
- At the end of the book, ask: "How did the author break this book into parts? Turn and talk about it with a partner."

MINILESSON Details

TEACH Display the minilesson principle on chart paper and read it aloud to children. Tell children they are going to learn to look for word and picture clues about how things look, feel, sound, and smell. Point out that this will help them understand what they read.

1. Discuss the principle with children, using examples from *How Animals Communicate*. Suggested language: "In the information book *How Animals Communicate*, we got clues about how animals look, feel, sound, and smell. Look at the elephants. What do you think their skin feels like? What clues tell you so?" *(It feels bumpy and rough. I think so because in the picture, the elephants have wrinkly skin.)*

> **MINILESSON PRINCIPLE**
>
> Notice the information that tells how things look, feel, sound, and smell.

2. Continue, using the bird as an example. Suggested language: "How do you think the bird sounds when it sings? What makes you think so?" *(I think the bird makes a soft, nice sound. I think so because the bird is small, so maybe it is not very loud. Also, the words say that the bird sings, so it must sound nice.)*

3. Use children's responses to the above question about the bird to fill in an Inference Map like the one shown here. Record what they think the bird might sound like in the big box at the bottom. Record the clues they used in boxes above.

Clue	Clue	Clue

SUMMARIZE AND APPLY Restate the minilesson principle. Then tell children to apply it to their independent reading. Suggested language: "When you read, look for information that tells how things look, feel, sound, and smell. Find clues in the words and pictures."

GROUP SHARE Ask children to share examples of information from another book they have read that tells how something looks, feels, sounds, or smells.

▶ Prairie Dogs

INTERACTIVE READ-ALOUD/SHARED READING

Read aloud the passage to children. Stop periodically for brief discussion. Use the following suggested stopping points and prompts:

- After you read the first paragraph, ask: "What do you think this will be about? What makes you think so?"
- After you read the section about how prairie dogs watch out for each other, ask: "What might cause prairie dogs to run for safety in their holes?"
- At the end, ask: "Do you think people should help to protect prairie dogs? Talk with a partner about your ideas."

MINILESSON Details

TEACH Display the minilesson principle on chart paper, and read it aloud to children. Tell children they are going to learn to use the author's words to figure out how things look.

1. Discuss with children what prairie dogs look like. Suggested language: "How big are prairie dogs?" *(They are the size of rabbits.)* Follow-up: "What other animals do you think they look like? What else do you know about how they look?" *(Answers will vary.)*

> **MINILESSON PRINCIPLE**
>
> Think about how the author uses describing words to tell how things look.

2. Reread the paragraph that begins *Prairie dogs live on prairies.* Tell children to listen for describing words as you read. Then ask: "Which words helped you get a picture of how prairie dogs look?" *(Possible answers include: brown/black fur; stubby tails; short, strong legs; sharp claws)*

3. Use the words children identified to fill in a Web with *Prairie Dogs* in the middle and words that tell what they look like in outside circles.

SUMMARIZE AND APPLY Restate the minilesson principle. Tell children to apply it to their independent reading. Suggested language: "When you read, pay attention to words that tell how things look."

GROUP SHARE Have children tell about describing words they found in their independent reading.

▶ Insect Messages

INTERACTIVE READ-ALOUD/SHARED READING

Read aloud the book to children. Stop periodically for brief discussion. Use the following suggested stopping points and prompts:

- After you read the first page, ask: "Do you think this book tells facts, or is it a made-up story? How do you know?"
- At the end of the book, ask: "What do the pictures show? Why do you think the author chose those pictures? Talk with a partner about your ideas."

MINILESSON Genre: Informational Text

TEACH Explain that *Insect Messages* is similar to the other two books they read this week because it contains facts and information.

1. Focus on *Insect Messages* to introduce the idea that the pictures and labels that go with informational texts contain important information. Suggested language: "*Insect Messages* has four pictures. What does each one show?" *(an insect that can send messages)*

> **MINILESSON PRINCIPLE**
>
> Look for important information in the pictures and the labels on the pictures.

2. Point out the label that goes with each picture and read it aloud. Ask: "How are the labels alike? What do they tell about the pictures?" *(They are each one word. They each give the name of the insect shown in the picture.)*

3. Write the minilesson principle on chart paper. Guide children to explain the important information they got from the words and pictures in *Insect Messages.* Explain that they will better understand what they read if they use the pictures and their labels to find important information.

SUMMARIZE AND APPLY Restate the minilesson principle. Tell children to apply it to their independent reading. Suggested language: "When you read, look for important information in pictures and labels."

GROUP SHARE Ask children to tell about pictures and labels in books they have read independently.

Whole-Group Lessons

A Musical Day
Student Book, Lesson 8

The Neighbors
Teacher's Edition, Lesson 8

Drums
Student Book, Lesson 8

▶ A Musical Day

INTERACTIVE READ-ALOUD/SHARED READING

Read aloud the story to children. Stop periodically for very brief discussion. Use the following suggested stopping points and prompts for quick group response, or give a specific prompt and have partners or threes turn and talk.

- After the children hug Aunt Viv, ask: "What is happening in the story?"
- After the children in the story yell *Yes!* with excitement, ask: "How do the children feel? Why do they feel that way?"
- After the two girls make guitars to pluck, ask: "What do the girls use to make their guitars? Find clues in the picture. Turn and talk about it with a partner."
- At the end of the story, ask: "What is the last thing that happened in this story?"

MINILESSON Sequence of Events

TEACH Display the minilesson principle on chart paper, and read it aloud to children. Tell children they are going to learn to think about what happens first and next in a story. Point out that this will help them understand the story better.

1. Discuss the principle with children, using examples from *A Musical Day*. Suggested language: "In the story *A Musical Day*, the first thing that happened was that Mom and Dad got ready for their trip. What happened next?" *(Aunt Viv arrived.)*

2. Have children name other story events in order. Suggested language: "What happened after the kids got a big hug from Aunt Viv?" *(They clapped, hopped, and sang.)*

3. Focus children's attention on the sequence of events in the story as a whole. Suggested language: "Now let's tell what happened in the whole story."

4. Ask children to tell about the whole story by explaining what happened first, next, and last. Record their ideas in a Flow Chart such as the one below.

> **MINILESSON PRINCIPLE**
>
> Think about what happens first and next in a story.

SUMMARIZE AND APPLY Restate the minilesson principle. Then tell children to apply it to their independent reading. Suggested language: "When you read, think about what happens first and next in a story."

GROUP SHARE Ask children to share what happened first and next in other stories they have read recently.

▶ The Neighbors

INTERACTIVE READ-ALOUD/SHARED READING

Read aloud the story to children. Stop periodically for brief discussion of the story. Use the following suggested stopping points and prompts:

- After you read the first paragraph, ask: "Where does this story happen? How do you know?"
- After Chen is interrupted by laughter from Li's house, ask: "How do you think Chen and Li are alike? How are they different?"
- At the end of the story, ask: "What important things happened in this story?"

MINILESSON Sequence of Events

TEACH Display the minilesson principle on chart paper, and read it aloud to children. Tell children they are going to use the order of what happened in a story to understand the story better.

1. Discuss with children the first important thing that happened in *The Neighbors*. Suggested language: "What happened first in the story?" *(Chen wanted to get rid of Li. He gave Li a box of gold coins.)*

> **MINILESSON PRINCIPLE**
>
> Think about the order of what happens in a story.

2. Have children discuss what happened next, or in the middle of the story. Suggested language: "What happened next?" *(Li spent all his time worrying about the money. Both he and his family were unhappy.)* Then work with children to tell what happened last, or at the end of the story. Ask: "What happened last?" *(Li gave back the money and learned a lesson.)*

3. Use children's responses to the above questions to fill in a Flow Chart for *The Neighbors*. Point out that a Flow Chart may not include every small thing that happened in the story, but the most important events should be shown in the order of first, next, and last.

SUMMARIZE AND APPLY Restate the minilesson principle. Tell children to apply it to their independent reading. Suggested language: "When you read, think about the order of what happens in a story."

GROUP SHARE Have children tell about the order of events in stories they read for independent reading.

▶ Drums

INTERACTIVE READ-ALOUD/SHARED READING

Read aloud the book to children. Stop periodically for brief discussion. Use the following suggested stopping points and prompts:

- After you read the first page, ask: "How do you think Yolanda Martinez feels about drums? How can you tell?"
- After you read the second page, ask: "What are some things all drums have?"
- After you read the last page, ask: "What are the steps to making a drum?"

MINILESSON Diagram

TEACH Explain to children that *Drums* has special parts that help readers because it includes photographs with labels. Tell them that the labeled pictures of drum parts help readers understand information that is not in the rest of the book.

1. Focus on the diagram in *Drums* to help children understand how pictures and labels can help them understand information. Suggested language: "What do the pictures show? How do the labels help tell about the pictures?" *(The picture shows three parts of a drum and each part's name.)*

> **MINILESSON PRINCIPLE**
>
> Think about how pictures and labels help you understand the information.

2. Write the minilesson principle on chart paper. Guide children to explain how the pictures and their labels helped them understand the different parts of a drum. Explain to children that pictures and their labels sometimes give information that is not found in other parts of a book.

SUMMARIZE AND APPLY Restate the minilesson principle. Tell children to apply it to their independent reading. Suggested language: "When you read, look at pictures and labels to help you understand important information."

GROUP SHARE Ask children to tell about pictures and labels in books they read for independent reading.

Whole-Group Lessons

Dr. Seuss
Student Book, Lesson 9

The Little Red Hen
Teacher's Edition, Lesson 9

Two Poems from Dr. Seuss
Student Book, Lesson 9

▶ Dr. Seuss

INTERACTIVE READ-ALOUD/SHARED READING

Read aloud the story to children. Stop periodically for very brief discussion of the story. Use the following suggested stopping points and prompts for quick group response, or give a specific prompt and have partners or threes turn and talk.

- After you read the page that says Ted was a funny man, ask: "How does the picture show that Ted was funny?"
- On the page that shows Dr. Seuss writing, ask: "Who is this story mostly about? How do you know?"
- On the page that shows Dr. Seuss reading to kids, ask: "Have you ever read or heard a Dr. Seuss story? What was it like?"
- At the end of the story, ask: "Why is Dr. Seuss famous today? Turn and talk about it with two partners."

MINILESSON Genre: Biography

TEACH Display the minilesson principle on chart paper, and read it aloud to children. Tell children that *Dr. Seuss* is a biography, or a story about a special person's life. In a biography, the author gives information to explain what makes that person special.

1. Discuss the principle with children, using examples from *Dr. Seuss*. Suggested language: "In the story *Dr. Seuss,* we learned that Ted wrote many books for children. How did this show that Ted was special?" *(Writing books is probably hard. Also, Ted drew pictures for his books. These things show that he was special.)*

2. Focus on other details from the story that show how Ted was special. Suggested language: "What was special about Ted's book *The Cat in the Hat?*" *(The main character is famous. Many people loved the book.)* Follow-up: "How did people feel about Ted's other books?" *(Many people loved his other books, too.)*

3. Create a Web such as the one shown below. In the center circle, write *Ways Ted Was Special*. Then use children's responses to the above questions to fill in the outer circles. If any circles are left blank, ask children to suggest other special things they learned about Ted from the story.

> **MINILESSON PRINCIPLE**
>
> Notice how the author tells what is special about the person she is writing about.

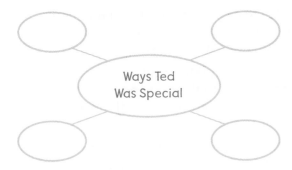

SUMMARIZE AND APPLY Restate the minilesson principle. Then tell children to apply it to their independent reading. Suggested language: "When you read, think about what makes the people you read about special."

GROUP SHARE Ask children to share something special about a person they have read about recently.

▶ The Little Red Hen

INTERACTIVE READ-ALOUD/SHARED READING

Read aloud the story to children. Stop periodically for brief discussion of the story. Use the following suggested stopping points and prompts:

- After you read the first paragraph of the story, ask: "Who are the important characters in the story so far?"
- After the duck, pig, and cat refuse to help take the wheat to the miller, ask: "Would you like to have the duck, pig, and cat as friends? Why or why not?"
- At the end of the story, ask: "How do you think the duck, pig, and cat feel at the end of the story? How do you think the Little Red Hen feels?"

MINILESSON Genre: Fairy Tale

TEACH Display the minilesson principle on chart paper, and read it aloud. Tell children that *The Little Red Hen* is a kind of story called a fairy tale. A fairy tale is a story about characters and things that could not happen in real life.

1. Discuss with children how the same thing happened over and over in the story. Suggested language: "How did the duck, pig, and cat answer every time the Little Red Hen asked for help?" *(Not I!)*

> **MINILESSON PRINCIPLE**
>
> Notice when the same thing happens over and over to think about what might happen next.

2. Review how the Little Red Hen asked for help planting the wheat, cutting the wheat, and taking it to the miller. Have children tell what they expected to happen when the Little Red Hen asked for help with the dough. Suggested language: "Did you think the other animals would help the Little Red Hen make her dough?" *(no)*

3. Help children understand that they should use clues, such as things that happen over and over, whenever they think about what might happen next in a story. Suggested language: "What made you think the duck, pig, and cat would not want to help the hen make her dough?" *(They said* no *to everything else she asked them to help with.)*

SUMMARIZE AND APPLY Restate the minilesson principle. Tell children to apply it to their independent reading. Suggested language: "When something happens over and over in a story, use this information to think about what might happen next."

GROUP SHARE Have children tell clues they used to guess what might happen next in stories from their independent reading.

▶ Two Poems from Dr. Seuss

INTERACTIVE READ-ALOUD/SHARED READING

Read aloud the introduction and poems to children. Stop periodically for brief discussion. Use the following suggested stopping points and prompts:

- After you read the first poem, say: "What was 'Pete Pats Pigs' about?"
- After you read the second poem, ask: "What was 'Quack Quack!' about?"
- Have children compare the two poems. "How were the poems the same? How were they different?"

MINILESSON Genre: Poetry

TEACH Remind children of ways that poems are different from other things they might read. Many poems rhyme, for example. Poems also include words that help readers make pictures in their minds. Then write the minilesson principle on chart paper, and read it aloud for children.

1. Have children close their eyes so they cannot see the pictures. Then reread "Pete Pats Pigs" for children, telling them to listen for words that help them picture Pete and his pigs. Suggested language: "Which words help you picture Pete? Which words help you picture the pigs and their playpen?" *(pink, big)*

> **MINILESSON PRINCIPLE**
>
> Think about how words in a poem make pictures in your mind.

2. Repeat the first step using the other poem, "Quack Quack!" Have children name words that help them picture each duck.

SUMMARIZE AND APPLY Restate the minilesson principle. Tell children to apply it to their independent reading. Suggested language: "When you read, think about how the author's words help you make pictures in your mind."

GROUP SHARE Ask children to tell about how they used words from their independent reading to make pictures in their minds.

Whole-Group Lessons

A Cupcake Party
Student Book, Lesson 10

Chipper Chips In
Teacher's Edition, Lesson 10

At the Bakery
Student Book, Lesson 10

▶ A Cupcake Party

INTERACTIVE READ-ALOUD/SHARED READING

Read aloud the story to children. Stop periodically for very brief discussion of the story. Use the following suggested stopping points and prompts for quick group response, or give a specific prompt and have partners or threes turn and talk.

- After Fritz says that he misses his friends, ask: "What do you think Fritz will do next?"
- On the page that shows Fritz putting cupcakes into the oven, ask: "What does Fritz do after he invites all his friends over for a party?"
- On the page that shows Fritz's friends giving him an acorn, ask: "Why do you think Fritz's friends brought him a snack?"
- At the end of the story, ask: "Do you think it would be fun to go to a party like Fritz's? Turn and talk about your ideas with a partner."

MINILESSON Story Structure

TEACH Display the minilesson principle on chart paper, and read it aloud to children. Explain that in most stories an important character has a problem. Tell children that they are going to learn to notice what problem a character has in a story and how he or she tries to solve it.

1. Discuss the principle with children, using examples from *A Cupcake Party*. Suggested language: "In the story *A Cupcake Party*, we learned that Fritz missed his friends. This was a problem. What was the first thing he did to try to solve this problem?" *(He decided to have a party.)*

2. Focus on the steps Fritz took to solve his problem. Suggested language: "What did Fritz do next to solve his problem?" *(He invited his friends to his party. Then he baked special cupcakes for his friends so the party would be fun.)*

3. Create a Flow Chart such as the one below to show Fritz's problem and what he did to solve it. In the top box, record Fritz's problem. Then use Fritz's ways of solving his problem to fill in the chart. Discuss how the chart shows both Fritz's problem and how he solved it.

> **MINILESSON PRINCIPLE**
>
> Notice how the characters in a story solve a problem.

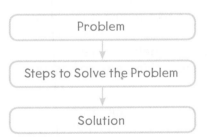

SUMMARIZE AND APPLY Restate the minilesson principle. Then tell children to apply it to their independent reading. Suggested language: "When you read, think about the problems that characters have and how they try to solve their problems."

GROUP SHARE Ask children to share a problem that a character faced in a story they read. Have them tell how the character solved his or her problem.

▶ Chipper Chips In

INTERACTIVE READ-ALOUD/SHARED READING

Read aloud the story to children. Stop periodically for brief discussion of the story. Use the following suggested stopping points and prompts:

- After Chipper's brothers tell her that she is too small to collect seeds, ask: "Who are the important characters in this story so far?"
- After the chipmunks are told that the first frost is coming soon, ask: "How do you think Chipper feels here? Why do you think so?"
- At the end of the story, ask: "What lesson do you think Chipper's brothers learned in the story? Turn and talk about your ideas with a partner."

MINILESSON Story Structure

TEACH Display the minilesson principle on chart paper and read it aloud to children. Tell children they are going to learn to notice the problems that different characters have in stories.

1. Discuss with children the problem that Chipper had at the beginning of *Chipper Chips In*. Suggested language: "What did Chipper's brothers tell her at the beginning of the story? How do you think that made her feel?" *(They told her that she was too small to help collect seeds for winter. That probably made her feel mad and left out.)*

> **MINILESSON PRINCIPLE**
>
> Notice that the characters in stories have problems to solve.

2. Help children understand that Chipper's problem was that her brothers did not want her to help. Suggested language: "What was Chipper's big problem?"

3. Explain to children that in some stories, more than one character has a problem. Use the example of the chipmunks needing to gather seeds quickly to help children understand. Suggested language: "In the middle of the story, all the chipmunks had a problem. What was it?" *(They needed to gather seeds very quickly.)*

SUMMARIZE AND APPLY Restate the minilesson principle. Tell children to apply it to their independent reading. Suggested language: "When you read, think about the problems that characters try to solve."

GROUP SHARE Ask children to share more examples from their independent reading of problems characters can have.

▶ At the Bakery

INTERACTIVE READ-ALOUD/SHARED READING

Read aloud the story to children. Stop periodically for brief discussion. Use the following suggested stopping points and prompts:

- After the baker asks for help, say: "What did the baker make?"
- After the baker explains that he needs help with the frosting, ask: "What happened before the baker asked the children to help make frosting?"
- After you read the recipe for frosting, ask: "What goes into the frosting? What do you think it will taste like when it is done?"

MINILESSON Directions

TEACH Explain to children that some books include information about how to do something. Then display the minilesson principle on chart paper and read it aloud.

1. Have children look back through *At the Bakery* to find information about how to do something. Suggested language: "The author of *At the Bakery* gave steps for how to do something. What do the steps show how to do?" *(how to make cupcake frosting)*

> **MINILESSON PRINCIPLE**
>
> Notice when the author is explaining how to do something.

2. Draw a Flow Chart with the headings *First, Next,* and *Last*. Have children name the steps to making frosting that were described in *At the Bakery*. Use this information to fill in the chart.

SUMMARIZE AND APPLY Restate the minilesson principle. Tell children to apply it to their independent reading. Suggested language: "When you read, look for places where the author explains how to do something."

GROUP SHARE Ask children to name other books or stories they have read that included information about how to do something.

Whole-Group Lessons

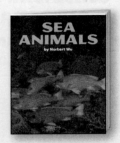

Sea Animals
Student Book, Lesson 11

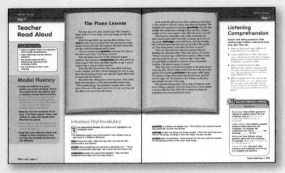

The Piano Lessons
Teacher's Edition, Lesson 11

Water
Student Book, Lesson 11

▶ Sea Animals

INTERACTIVE READ-ALOUD/SHARED READING

Read aloud the book to children. Stop periodically for very brief discussion of it. Use the following suggested stopping points and prompts for quick group response, or give a specific prompt and have partners or threes turn and talk.

- After the ghost pipefish, ask: "What do the words in dark type under the pictures tell you?"
- After the California sea lions, ask: "Do you think a sea slug could live where the sea lions live? Why or why not?"
- After the sea turtle, ask: "Why do you think this turtle moves more slowly on land?"
- At the end of the selection, ask: "How are sea animals the same? How are they different? Turn and talk about your ideas with a partner."

MINILESSON Author's Purpose

TEACH Display the minilesson principle on chart paper, and read it aloud to children. Tell children they are going to think about how authors can write to give information.

> **MINILESSON PRINCIPLE**
>
> Think about how authors sometimes write to give information.

1. Discuss the principle with children, using *Sea Animals* as an example. Suggested language: "There are different kinds of books. Some books tell stories. Other books give information or tell about real things. What kind of book is *Sea Animals?*" *(an information book)* Follow-up: "How do you know?" *(It gives information about sea animals.)*

2. Focus on one part of the selection, such as the four pages that discuss where sea animals live. Suggested language: "This book tells about different places a sea animal can live. Think about two different sea animals and where they live. What information did the author give?" *(Penguins can live where it is cold. Sea lions can live where it is warm.)*

3. Use children's responses to explain that authors have different reasons for writing. Suggested language: "The author of *Sea Animals* wrote it for a reason. You can see that each page in the book gives information about sea animals. This helps you figure out that the author wrote it to give information."

4. Elicit from children additional facts from the text. Record children's ideas in an Inference Map like the one shown here.

SUMMARIZE AND APPLY Restate the minilesson principle. Then tell children to apply it to their independent reading. Suggested language: "When you read a book, think about why the author wrote it. Does the book give information or was it written for a different reason?"

GROUP SHARE Have children share why they think the author wrote the book they are reading. Ask them to share details from the book that support their ideas.

▶ The Piano Lessons

INTERACTIVE READ-ALOUD/SHARED READING

Read aloud the story to children. Stop periodically for brief discussion of it. Use the following suggested stopping points and prompts:

- After the first page, ask: "How would you describe Mrs. Johnson? What does she say and do to help you figure out what she is like?"
- After Mrs. Johnson suggests that the girls practice together, ask: "Did Mrs. Johnson surprise you here? Why or why not?"
- At the end of the story, say: "How has Kim changed from the beginning of the story to the end? Turn and talk with a partner about how and why she changed."

MINILESSON Author's Purpose

TEACH Display the minilesson principle on chart paper, and read it aloud to children. Tell children they are going to think about how authors can write stories for readers to enjoy.

1. Discuss the principle with children, using *The Piano Lessons* as an example. Focus on one part of the story, such as when Kim is practicing in the beginning. Suggested language: "The author helps you create a picture in your mind as you listen to the story. You heard the words *plink, plonk, thud*. These helped you understand how terrible Kim was at practicing and might have made you laugh. What did Kim say about practicing that sounded like a real girl talking?" *(This is soooo boring.)*

> **MINILESSON PRINCIPLE**
>
> Think about how authors sometimes write to help readers enjoy their stories.

2. Use children's responses to explain that authors have different reasons for writing. Suggested language: "You can tell that the author of *The Piano Lessons* wants you to laugh at this part. This helps you figure out that the author wrote the story for readers to enjoy."

3. Help children identify other parts of the story that help them understand the author's purpose. Write their ideas in an Inference Map.

SUMMARIZE AND APPLY Restate the minilesson principle. Tell children to apply it to their independent reading. Suggested language: "When you read, think about what the author does to help you enjoy the book."

GROUP SHARE Have children share why they think the author wrote the book that they read independently. Ask them to share details from the book that show how the author helped them enjoy the story.

▶ Water

INTERACTIVE READ-ALOUD/SHARED READING

Read aloud the book to children. Stop periodically for brief discussion of it. Use the following suggested stopping points and prompts:

- After the first page, ask: "What is a liquid? How does the picture help you understand the words?"
- At the end, ask: "How is liquid water different from frozen water? Turn and talk about your ideas with a partner."

MINILESSON Genre: Informational Text

TEACH Explain to children that two of the books they read this week, *Sea Animals* and *Water,* were written to give information.

1. Focus on the first two pages to introduce how authors can make information interesting. Suggested language: "In *Water*, the author used different kinds of sentences. The first part has questions and answers. This can make information more interesting to read."

> **MINILESSON PRINCIPLE**
>
> Notice how authors make information interesting.

2. Explain that the author of *Water* also used pictures to give information. Tell children that pictures are often used to make information more interesting.

3. Ask children to share parts of *Water* that they found interesting. Write the minilesson principle on chart paper. Guide children to identify features, such as diagrams and pictures, that make information interesting.

SUMMARIZE AND APPLY Restate the minilesson principle. Tell children to apply it to their independent reading. Suggested language: "When you read, think about how the author keeps you interested in the information you are reading."

GROUP SHARE Ask children to share a part of a book they chose for independent reading. Have them tell how the author made it interesting.

Whole-Group Lessons

How Leopard Got His Spots
Student Book, Lesson 12

Turtle, Frog, and Rat
Teacher's Edition, Lesson 12

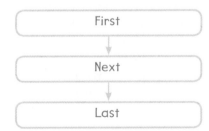

The Rain Forest
Student Book, Lesson 12

▶ How Leopard Got His Spots

INTERACTIVE READ-ALOUD/SHARED READING

Read aloud the story to children. Stop periodically for very brief discussion of it. Use the following suggested stopping points and prompts for quick group response, or give a specific prompt and have partners or threes turn and talk.

- After Fred gets stuck, ask: "Why do you think Fred felt very sad? How do you think he feels about Hal?"
- After Fred paints Zel and Jill, ask: "How do you think Leopard will get his spots?"
- After Hal says *Paint me, too,* ask: "What do you think Fred will do? Turn and talk with your partner about what you think will happen next."
- At the end of the story, ask: "What lesson can you learn from this story?" Follow-up: "Has anyone ever played a trick on you? How did it make you feel?"

MINILESSON Sequence of Events

TEACH Display the minilesson principle on chart paper, and read it aloud to children. Tell children they are going to learn how to think about order as they read. Explain that most stories happen in a certain order. They tell what happens first, next, and last.

1. Discuss the principle with children, using events from the first part of *How Leopard Got His Spots.* Suggested language: "In the story *How Leopard Got His Spots,* things happen in order. Let's look at the first five pages of the story. What happened first?" *(Hal and Fred were playing catch, and Hal tricked Fred.)*

2. Focus on what happened directly after Hal tricked Fred. Suggested language: "What happened to Fred after he got tricked?" *(He got stuck in the plant and yelled for help.)* "What happened last?" *(Len cut the plants and let Fred out.)*

3. Use children's responses to explain how authors put events in an order that makes sense. Suggested language: "The author told what happened first, next, and last. When you think about the order in which things happen, it helps you understand the story."

4. Work with children to sequence the most important events from the whole story. Record children's ideas in a flow chart like the one shown here.

> **MINILESSON PRINCIPLE**
>
> Think about what happens first, next, and last in a story.

```
┌─────────────────┐
│      First      │
└─────────────────┘
         │
         ▼
┌─────────────────┐
│      Next       │
└─────────────────┘
         │
         ▼
┌─────────────────┐
│      Last       │
└─────────────────┘
```

SUMMARIZE AND APPLY Restate the minilesson principle. Explain to children that they can apply it to their independent reading. Suggested language: "When you read a story, think about what happens first, next, and last."

GROUP SHARE Have children share the sequence of events from a story they read for independent reading. Ask them to tell what happened first, next, and last.

▶ Turtle, Frog, and Rat

INTERACTIVE READ-ALOUD/SHARED READING

Read aloud the story to children. Stop periodically for brief discussion of it. Use the following suggested stopping points and prompts:

- After the animals compliment each other, ask: "Do you think Rat, Turtle, and Frog are good friends to each other? Why or why not?"
- After Rat finds his friends, ask: "How do you think Rat feels when he finds his friends?" Follow-up: "How do you think Turtle and Frog feel when they see Rat?"
- At the end of the story, say: "What lesson can you learn from Rat's wife? Turn and talk with a partner about whether you think it is a good lesson."

MINILESSON Genre: Folktale

TEACH Display the minilesson principle on chart paper, and read it aloud to children. Tell children they are going to learn to think about how a folktale can explain something in nature.

1. Focus on *Turtle, Frog, and Rat* to introduce the idea that some folktales explain why things in nature came to be. Suggested language: "In the story *Turtle, Rat, and Frog,* the animals changed. What did each animal look like at the beginning of the story?" (*Frog had flat eyes. Turtle had a smooth shell. Rat had a furry tail.*)

> **MINILESSON PRINCIPLE**
>
> Notice that a folktale explains why something is the way it is.

2. Use children's responses to point out how this folktale explains why something is the way it is. Suggested language: "You know that today these animals look different. Frogs have bulging eyes, turtles have rough shells, and rats have skinny, furless tails. How did the story explain why this is?" (*The animals had an accident when they were trying to meet Rat's wife.*)

3. As children share the events that led to each animal's appearance, write the minilesson principle on chart paper. Explain to children that some folktales have funny ways of explaining things in nature.

SUMMARIZE AND APPLY Restate the minilesson principle. Tell children to apply it to their independent reading. Suggested language: "When you read a folktale, look for ways it explains why something is the way it is."

GROUP SHARE Ask children to summarize folktales they have read that tell why something is the way it is.

▶ The Rain Forest

INTERACTIVE READ-ALOUD/SHARED READING

Read aloud the book to children. Stop periodically for brief discussion of it. Use the following suggested stopping points and prompts:

- After the understory paragraph, ask: "Why is the understory layer shady?"
- After the forest floor paragraph, ask: "Which part of the rainforest do you think has the largest animals? Why?"
- At the end of the selection, ask: "How do the pictures, labels, and map help you better understand the information? Turn and talk about your ideas with a partner."

MINILESSON Genre: Informational Text

TEACH Explain to children that *The Rain Forest* is different from the other two stories they read this week. Point out that it gives information about a real place.

1. Focus on the headings to introduce how authors call attention to information. Suggested language: "In *The Rain Forest,* the author included some words in red type. These words are also darker than the words around them."

> **MINILESSON PRINCIPLE**
>
> Think about why the author made the letters different colors and sizes.

2. Page through the text with children to identify the three headings in red, bold type. Point out how each heading tells what the paragraph is going to be about. Suggested language: "Look at the words *Canopy Layer.* They are a different color and bigger than the words around them. If you read the sentences that follow it, you can see that they all tell about the canopy layer. If you want to find information about a part of the rain forest, you can easily find it by looking for the words in red that name the part."

3. Write the minilesson principle on chart paper. Guide children to see how the headings stand out from the other words. Explain to children that authors put words in different colors or sizes to draw a reader's attention to them or to help them find information.

SUMMARIZE AND APPLY Restate the minilesson principle. Explain to children that they can apply it to their independent reading. Suggested language: "When you read, look for words that are shown in different colors or sizes from the rest of the words in the book."

GROUP SHARE Ask children to share examples of words shown in special colors or sizes in a book they read.

Whole-Group Lessons

Seasons
Student Book, Lesson 13

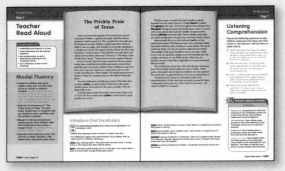

The Prickly Pride of Texas
Teacher's Edition, Lesson 13

The Four Seasons
Student Book, Lesson 13

▶ Seasons

INTERACTIVE READ-ALOUD/SHARED READING

Read aloud the book to children. Stop periodically for very brief discussion of it. Use the following suggested stopping points and prompts for quick group response, or give a specific prompt and have partners or threes turn and talk.

- After the last page of the Spring section, ask: "How do the words on this page help you make a picture in your mind of what spring is like?"
- After the last page of the Fall section, ask: "Why do you think animals pack away nuts in the fall?"
- At the end, ask: "Why do you think the author chose to write this information like a poem? Turn and talk to a partner about whether or not this was a good way to learn about the seasons."

MINILESSON Cause and Effect

TEACH Display the minilesson principle on chart paper, and read it aloud to children. Tell children they are going to learn how to notice how one thing can make another thing happen. Explain that understanding why things happen will help them better understand a whole story.

1. Discuss the principle with children, using examples from *Seasons*. Suggested language: "In the Spring section of *Seasons*, you read that the grass made a squish sound. What happened to make the grass squish?" *(It rained, and the grass got wet.)*

2. Use children's responses to explain how to notice when one thing causes another. Suggested language: "The rain made the grass squish. The rain was one thing that made another thing happen. As you read, it is important to look for the reasons why things happen."

3. Work with children to find events that made other things happen. Record children's ideas in a T-Map like the one shown here.

> **MINILESSON PRINCIPLE**
>
> Notice when one thing makes another thing happen.

What Happened?	Why?

SUMMARIZE AND APPLY Restate the minilesson principle. Explain to children that they can apply it to their independent reading. Suggested language: "When you read a story, notice how one thing can make another thing happen."

GROUP SHARE Have children share an example of one thing that made another thing happen from their independent reading.

▶ The Prickly Pride of Texas

INTERACTIVE READ-ALOUD/SHARED READING

Read aloud the selection to children. Stop periodically for brief discussion of it. Use the following suggested stopping points and prompts:

- After the retelling of the legend, ask: "Why do you think the author began this with a story?"
- After the paragraph that describes how parts of the plant can be used for food, say: "Turn and talk with a partner about how different parts of prickly pear cactus might taste." Follow-up: "Do you think you would like to eat any parts of the prickly pear cactus? If you have before, what was it like?"
- At the end, ask: "How does the author feel about the prickly pear cactus? How can you tell?"

MINILESSON Genre: Informational Text

TEACH Display the minilesson principle on chart paper, and read it aloud to children. Tell children they are going to think about words the author used to tell what the prickly pear cactus is like.

1. Tell children that authors often use words that help readers picture what something is like. Suggested language: "In *The Prickly Pride of Texas,* the author used words that help you understand what the plant is like. These words told about how the cactus looks, feels, and tastes. Do you remember what the author said the leaves looked like?" *(flat, green paddles shaped like tears)*

> **MINILESSON PRINCIPLE**
>
> Notice when an author tells what something is like.

2. Work with children to find other descriptive details from the story. Write their ideas in a Web with *Prickly Pear Cactus* in the center circle. Have children suggest details that tell about the cactus in the outer circles.

SUMMARIZE AND APPLY Restate the minilesson principle. Explain to children that they should apply it to their independent reading. Suggested language: "When you read, pay attention to words that tell what something is like."

GROUP SHARE Have children choose a description they have read in a book. Ask them to share words the author used to tell what something is like. You may wish to have the group tell which words helped them best picture the thing being described.

▶ The Four Seasons

INTERACTIVE READ-ALOUD/SHARED READING

Read aloud the introduction and poems to children. Stop periodically for brief discussion of the poems. Use the following suggested stopping points and prompts:

- After the poem "Spring Song," ask: "What is saying *Here comes Spring!* in the poem? Is this something that could really happen? Turn and talk about your ideas with a partner."
- After the poem "Listen," ask: "What makes the sound *scrunch, crunch* in the poem? What do you picture in your mind when you hear this?"

MINILESSON Genre: Poetry

TEACH Remind children that they have read three poems: "Spring Song," "Listen," and "Seasons Song." Explain that some poems have words that can make you feel a certain way.

1. Read aloud the last two lines of "Spring Song," emphasizing a feeling of excitement. Have children follow along. Point out that these sentences each have an exclamation mark at the end. Ask: "How do you feel when you hear these words?" *(happy, excited)*

> **MINILESSON PRINCIPLE**
>
> Think about how the words in poems make you feel.

2. Help children notice other words that convey feelings. Read aloud the first line of "Listen." Ask: "In this poem, do these words have a happy sound or an angry sound?" *(happy)* "What other feelings do these sound words give you?"

3. Ask children to share feelings they have had about these and other poems they have read. Prompt children to recognize the words in the poem that helped create these feelings as you write the minilesson principle on chart paper. Explain to children that thinking about their feelings as they read a poem will help them enjoy it more.

SUMMARIZE AND APPLY Restate the minilesson principle. Tell children to apply it to their independent reading. Suggested language: "When you read poems, think about how the words make you feel."

GROUP SHARE Ask children to share words from poems and tell how they make them feel. Have them explain why the words make them feel a certain way.

Whole-Group Lessons

The Big Race
Student Book, Lesson 14

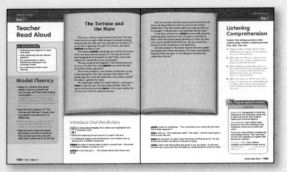

The Tortoise and the Hare
Teacher's Edition, Lesson 14

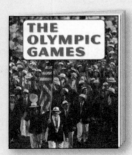

The Olympic Games
Student Book, Lesson 14

▶ The Big Race

INTERACTIVE READ-ALOUD/SHARED READING

Read aloud the story to children. Stop periodically for very brief discussion of it. Use the following suggested stopping points and prompts for quick group response, or give a specific prompt and have partners or threes turn and talk.

- After Red Lizard gets to the race, ask: "What is special about the race? Why does Red Lizard want to run in it?"
- After all the animals arrive at the starting line, ask: "Who is running in this race? Who do you think will win? Why do you think this?"
- After Roadrunner trips over the rake, ask: "Who do you think will win the race now? Turn and talk with your partner about who you think will win."
- At the end of the story, ask: "What lesson can you learn from this story?" Follow-up: "When have you shared something with your friends?"

MINILESSON Conclusions

TEACH Display the minilesson principle on chart paper, and read it aloud to children. Tell children they are going to learn how to notice clues about characters as they read. Explain that the clues will help them figure out what a character is like.

1. Discuss the principle with children, using examples of characters from *The Big Race*. Suggested language: "In *The Big Race*, five characters ran in the race. Which character finished the race?" (*Red Lizard*) "What happened to the other characters?" (*They either fell or stopped paying attention*.)

2. Focus on the character Red Lizard. Suggested language: "Red Lizard won the race and the cake. Do you remember what he did with his prize?" (*At first, he was going to eat the cake all by himself. Then he saw that his pals looked sad. He decided to share the cake with his pals.*)

3. Use children's responses to explain how authors give clues about what characters are like. Suggested language: "What Red Lizard did at the end shows you that he was kind and generous. The author did not tell you that Red Lizard was kind, but you can figure it out because of what he did."

4. Work with children to draw conclusions about other characters in the story. Record children's ideas in an Inference Map like the one shown here.

> **MINILESSON PRINCIPLE**
>
> Notice clues about characters to help you understand what they are like.

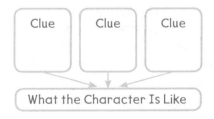

SUMMARIZE AND APPLY Restate the minilesson principle. Explain to children that they can apply it to their independent reading. Suggested language: "When you read a story, think about what the characters are like. Look for clues that the author tells you about them."

GROUP SHARE Have children share a description of one character in a story they read for independent reading. Ask them to tell what the character is like. Then have them give clues from the story that helped them figure out what the character is like.

▶ The Tortoise and the Hare

INTERACTIVE READ-ALOUD/SHARED READING

Read aloud the story to children. Stop periodically for brief discussion of it. Use the following suggested stopping points and prompts:

- After the tortoise challenges the hare to a race, ask: "Why do you think the tortoise wants to race the hare?"
- After the hare sits down, ask: "Why does the hare decide to take a rest?" Follow-up: "Do you think this is a good idea? Why or why not?"
- At the end of the story, say: "Think about what the coyote says. Do you think it is a good lesson? Turn and talk about your ideas with a partner."

MINILESSON Conclusions

TEACH Display the minilesson principle on chart paper, and read it aloud to children. Tell children they are going to learn to use what characters say and do to figure out what they are like.

1. Remind children how authors give clues about what characters are like. Explain that clues can be what a character says and does. Suggested language: "In the story *The Tortoise and the Hare,* what did the hare do when the tortoise asked him to race?" (*The hare laughed. He said there was no one faster.*)

> **MINILESSON PRINCIPLE**
>
> Think about what characters say and what they do to help you know what they are like.

2. Point out to children that what characters say and what they do help you know what they are like. Suggested language: "The author used what the hare said—when he bragged to the tortoise—and what he did— laughed—to show you what the hare was like. You can figure out that the hare was sure of himself and thought he could not lose."

3. Work with children to draw additional conclusions about tortoise from the story. Write their ideas in an Inference Map.

SUMMARIZE AND APPLY Restate the minilesson principle. Explain to children that they should apply it to their independent reading. Suggested language: "When you read, think about what characters say and what they do to figure out what they are like."

GROUP SHARE Have children choose a character from a story and tell what the character said and did. Then have them tell what the character was like.

▶ The Olympic Games

INTERACTIVE READ-ALOUD/SHARED READING

Read aloud the book to children. Stop periodically for brief discussion of it. Use the following suggested stopping points and prompts:

- After the first paragraph, ask: "What are *athletes*? How did you figure it out?"
- At the end of the second page, ask: "What is the same about Eric Heiden and Carl Lewis? Talk about your ideas with a partner."
- At the end, ask: "Which athlete would you like to read more about? Why?"

MINILESSON Genre: Informational Text

TEACH Explain to children that *The Olympic Games* is different from the other two stories they read this week. Point out that it gives information about real people, places, and events.

1. Focus on the captions to introduce how authors give information about pictures. Suggested language: "In *The Olympic Games*, the author included some sentences in dark type. These sentences tell more about the picture below or beside it."

> **MINILESSON PRINCIPLE**
>
> Notice the words and sentences authors use to tell about the pictures.

2. Page through the book with children to identify two captions and what each one explains about a picture. Then write the minilesson principle on chart paper. Guide children to see how the captions are different from the main part of a book. Help them recognize that sometimes words that tell about pictures give extra information that may not be found in the main part of a book. Explain to children that paying attention to special type and words that appear near pictures will help them read all the information that the author is sharing with them.

SUMMARIZE AND APPLY Restate the minilesson principle. Explain to children that they can apply it to their independent reading. Suggested language: "When you read, look for special words and sentences that tell about pictures."

GROUP SHARE Ask children to share examples of words that told about pictures in a book they read.

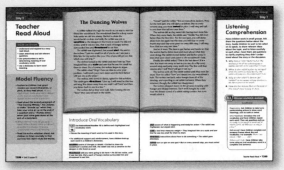

Animal Groups
Student Book, Lesson 15

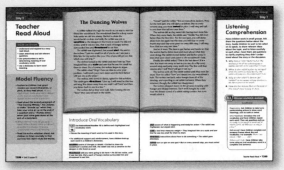

The Dancing Wolves
Teacher's Edition, Lesson 15

Animal Picnic
Student Book, Lesson 15

▶ Animal Groups

INTERACTIVE READ-ALOUD/SHARED READING

Read aloud the book to children. Stop periodically for very brief discussion of it. Use the following suggested stopping points and prompts for quick group response, or give a specific prompt and have partners or threes turn and talk.

- After the section about fish, ask: "Why do fish have gills?" Follow-up: "What is different about the way you breathe?"
- After the section about reptiles, ask: "What are some of the different ways that reptiles move around?"
- After the bird section, ask: "What are some animals that hatch from eggs?"
- At the end of the book, ask: "What is the same about all mammals? Turn and talk about your ideas with a partner."

MINILESSON Compare and Contrast

TEACH Display the minilesson principle on chart paper, and read it aloud to children. Tell children they are going to learn how to think about the ways in which things can be the same and different.

> **MINILESSON PRINCIPLE**
>
> Think about how things are the same and how they are different.

1. Discuss the principle with children, using *Animals Groups* as an example. Suggested language: "In *Animal Groups*, you learned about five different animal groups. The animals in each group are the same in some ways. What is the same about all amphibians?" (*They have wet skin. They live on land and water. They hatch from eggs.*)

2. Then choose another animal group for children to compare to amphibians. Suggested language: "Can you remember what is the same about all birds?" (*They have feathers and wings. They hatch from eggs.*)

3. Use children's responses to explain how to compare and contrast. Suggested language: "Think about the two animal groups Amphibians and Birds. How are they the same? How are they different?" (*They are the same because they both hatch from eggs. They are different because amphibians have wet skin, but birds have feathers and wings.*)

4. Work with children to tell how two of the animal groups are the same and different. Record children's ideas in a Venn Diagram like the one shown here.

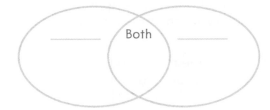

SUMMARIZE AND APPLY Restate the minilesson principle. Explain to children that they can apply it to their independent reading. Suggested language: "When you read a book, think about how things are the same and different."

GROUP SHARE Have children tell about how two different books they read were the same and different.

▶ The Dancing Wolves

INTERACTIVE READ-ALOUD/SHARED READING

Read aloud the story to children. Stop periodically for brief discussion of it. Use the following suggested stopping points and prompts:

- After the rabbit suggests a dance contest, ask: "What is rabbit like?" Follow-up: "Do you really think he is giving himself up as a prize? What do you think will happen next?"
- At the end of the story, ask: "Why do you think the author wrote this story? How do you know? Turn and talk about your ideas with a partner."

MINILESSON Story Structure

TEACH Display the minilesson principle on chart paper, and read it aloud to children. Tell children they are going to think about characters and what has happened in a story to figure out what might happen next.

1. Explain to children that authors sometimes give clues about what might happen next in a story. Use *The Dancing Wolves* as an example. Suggested language: "In *The Dancing Wolves*, what did the rabbit do after the wolves finished the first dance?" (*He moved farther away and gave the wolves a harder dance to do.*) Follow-up: "What did the rabbit do after the wolves finished the second dance?" (*He moved even father away and gave the wolves an even harder dance.*)

> **MINILESSON PRINCIPLE**
>
> Think about the characters and what happened to think what might happen next.

2. Remind children that they can make guesses about what might happen next using what they know about the characters and events in a story. Suggested language: "As you listened, you heard that the rabbit moved farther away with each dance. This is a good clue that rabbit will get away in the end. Because the author gave the story a pattern, it helped you make a good guess about what would happen next."

SUMMARIZE AND APPLY Restate the minilesson principle. Explain to children that they should apply it to their independent reading. Suggested language: "When you read, think about what characters say and do and what happens to figure out what might happen next."

GROUP SHARE Have children tell about the events in a book they are reading. If they have not finished, have them tell what they think might happen next and explain why. If they have finished, have them tell what they thought would happen while reading and whether or not it was correct.

▶ Animal Picnic

INTERACTIVE READ-ALOUD/SHARED READING

Read aloud the play to children. Stop periodically for brief discussion of it. Use the following suggested stopping points and prompts:

- After Bird says *I had to fly to get here,* ask: "How did each animal get to the picnic. How do you know?"
- At the end of the play, ask: "Do you think the animals will try eating each other's food? Turn and talk about your ideas with a partner."

MINILESSON Compare and Contrast

TEACH Remind children that it is important to think about how things are the same and different as they read. Point out that they can think about how characters are the same and different to help them better understand a story.

1. Discuss the principle with children, using Fox and Cow as an example. Suggested language: "In *Animal Picnic*, the animals Fox, Cow, and Bird all meet for a picnic. What is the same about Cow and Fox?" (*They both brought food to the picnic. They both have teeth.*)

> **MINILESSON PRINCIPLE**
>
> Think about how the characters in a story are the same and how they are different.

2. Use children's responses to explain how to contrast. Suggested language: "Think about Fox and Cow's food and teeth. How are Fox and Cow different?" (*Cow brought grass and has flat teeth. Fox brought meat and has sharp teeth.*)

3. Work with children to compare and contrast Bird to either Fox or Cow. Record children's ideas in a Venn Diagram.

SUMMARIZE AND APPLY Restate the minilesson principle. Explain to children that they can apply it to their independent reading. Suggested language: "When you read, think about how characters are the same and different."

GROUP SHARE Ask children to share how characters in a book they read were the same and different.

Whole-Group Lessons

Let's Go to the Moon!
Student Book, Lesson 16

One Giant Leap
Teacher's Edition, Lesson 16

Mae Jemison
Student Book, Lesson 16

▶ Let's Go to the Moon!

INTERACTIVE READ-ALOUD/SHARED READING

Read aloud the book to children. Stop periodically for very brief discussion of the text. Use the following suggested stopping points and prompts for quick group response, or give a specific prompt and have partners or threes turn and talk.

- After reading the section called Blast Off!, ask: "Where is the space ship going? How do you know?"
- After reading the page titled Moon Rocks, ask: "How do the words *Moon Rocks* look different from other words in the book? What information do they help you find?"
- After reading about Taking Pictures, ask: "Who is telling about the Moon and the events that happened there? How do you know?"
- At the end of the book, ask: "Would like to visit the Moon? Why or why not? Turn and talk about your ideas with a partner."

MINILESSON Main Idea and Details

TEACH Display the minilesson principle on chart paper, and read it aloud to children. Tell children they are going to learn how to think about the most important idea in a book as they read.

> **MINILESSON PRINCIPLE**
>
> Notice that an author tells mostly about one idea and tells information about the idea.

1. Discuss the principle with children, using examples of main ideas from *Let's Go to the Moon!* Suggested language: "*Let's Go to the Moon!* is mostly about one idea. What is the book mostly about?" *(The book is mostly about astronauts visiting the Moon.)*

2. Focus on one detail that supports the main idea, such as the details in the Moon Walk section. Suggested language: "In the section called Moon Walk, the author told about astronauts walking on the Moon. What did you learn about walking on the Moon?" *(People and things are light on the Moon because there is less gravity.)*

3. Use children's responses to explain how details tell more information about the main idea of the book. Suggested language: "The information about Moon walks told us more about what it is like when astronauts visit the Moon."

4. Elicit additional details from the story. Record children's ideas in a Web like the one shown here.

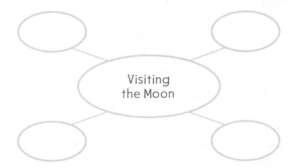

SUMMARIZE AND APPLY Restate the minilesson principle. Then tell children to apply it to their independent reading. Suggested language: "When you read, think about what the book is mostly about. Think about how the other information tells about that idea."

GROUP SHARE Ask children to talk about a book from their independent reading by telling what it is mostly about. Have them explain how information in the book tells about that idea.

▶ One Giant Leap

INTERACTIVE READ-ALOUD/SHARED READING

Read aloud the book to children. Stop periodically for brief discussion of the text. Use the following suggested stopping points and prompts:

- After the first paragraph, ask: "Who were the first two people to land on the Moon?"
- After the second paragraph, ask: "What was the purpose of the *Apollo 11* project?"
- At the end of the book, ask: "How were Armstrong's and Aldrin's visit to the Moon the same as Collins's? How were they different?"

MINILESSON Main Ideas and Details

TEACH Display the minilesson principle on chart paper, and read it aloud to children. Tell children that they are going to learn to think about what a book is mostly about.

1. Using the events from *One Giant Leap*, discuss with children that a book is mostly about one thing. Suggested language: "In *One Giant Leap*, you read about the *Apollo 11* astronauts. What special thing did they do?" *(They went to the Moon. Two of them were the first people to land on the Moon.)*

> **MINILESSON PRINCIPLE**
>
> Notice what the book is mostly about.

2. Talk with children about the events that took the astronauts to the Moon. Suggested language: "The astronauts' adventure began on July 16, 1969. What happened on that date?" *(The spaceship blasted off.)* Follow-up: "What were the important things that happened over the next four days?" *(The astronauts traveled to the Moon. Armstrong and Aldrin landed a small craft on the Moon.)*

3. Tell children that all the ideas in a book will help them notice what a book is mostly about. In an Idea-Support Map, write some of the details that children have mentioned. Then guide them to tell what all the details are mostly about, and write the main idea in the top box.

SUMMARIZE AND APPLY Restate the minilesson principle. Tell children to apply it to their independent reading. Suggested language: "When you read, think about what the book is mostly about to help you understand it."

GROUP SHARE Ask children to tell what a book they are reading is mostly about.

▶ Mae Jemison

INTERACTIVE READ-ALOUD/SHARED READING

Read aloud the book to children. Stop periodically for brief discussion of the text. Use the following suggested stopping points and prompts:

- After the first page, ask: "Who is this book about? Why is she special?"
- At the end of the book, have children look at the timeline: "In what year did Mae become an astronaut?" Follow-up: "Did Mae become an astronaut before or after she started her company? How does the timeline help you know?"

MINILESSON Genre: Biography

TEACH Remind children that they have read three stories this week: *Let's Go to the Moon!, One Giant Step,* and *Mae Jemison.* Explain that the stories have something in common—they are information books that tell about astronauts and the events in their lives.

1. Focus on *Mae Jemison* to introduce the idea that a biography tells about the events in a person's life. Suggested language: "The book *Mae Jemison* is a biography that told about a real person, Mae Jemison. It told where she was born and what she wanted to be. As you read biographies, think about the important things that happened in the real person's life."

> **MINILESSON PRINCIPLE**
>
> Think about the important things that happen in a person's life.

2. Ask children to share some of the important things that Mae Jemison did in her life. Suggested language: "What are some important things that happened in Mae Jemison's life?" *(She became a doctor and an astronaut; she started a company.)*

3. Guide children to summarize the events as you write the minilesson principle on chart paper.

SUMMARIZE AND APPLY Restate the minilesson principle. Tell children to apply it to their independent reading. Suggested language: "When you read a biography, look for the important events that happen in a person's life."

GROUP SHARE Ask children to retell the important things that happen in a person's life from the book they read for independent reading.

The Big Trip
Student Book, Lesson 17

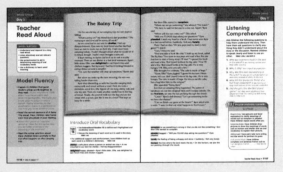

The Rainy Trip
Teacher's Edition, Lesson 17

Lewis and Clark's Big Trip
Student Book, Lesson 17

▶ The Big Trip

INTERACTIVE READ-ALOUD/SHARED READING

Read aloud the story to children. Stop periodically for very brief discussion of the text. Use the following suggested stopping points and prompts for quick group response, or give a specific prompt and have partners or threes turn and talk.

- After Pig and Goat discuss taking a trip by bike, ask: "Who are the characters in the story?" Before continuing the story, say: "Listen to see if Goat changes during this story."
- After Pig suggests taking a trip by donkey, ask: "Why does Pig think taking a donkey cart is a good idea? Why does Goat think it is a bad idea?"
- At the end of the story, ask: "How has Goat changed during this story? What makes you think so?" Follow-up: "Do you like to take trips? How do you like to get where you are going? Why?"

MINILESSON Compare and Contrast

TEACH Display the minilesson principle on chart paper, and read it aloud to children. Tell children they are going to learn how to think about how things in a story are the same and different. Explain that they will use story clues to help them.

1. Discuss the principle with children, using examples from *The Big Trip*. Suggested language: "In the story *The Big Trip*, Pig had the idea to take his trip by plane and hot air balloon. How are these two ways of taking a trip the same?" *(They travel in the air.)* "How are they different?" *(A plane is a metal frame lifted by an engine. A hot air balloon is a basket lifted by a balloon.)*

2. Focus on the hot air balloon. Suggested language: "How did Pig feel about taking a trip in a hot air balloon?" *(Pig thought it was a good idea because it would get him where he wanted to go.)* "How did Goat feel about it?" *(Goat worried that the balloon would get a hole.)*

3. Use children's responses to explain how authors show that things in a story, such as characters, places, or things, are the same and different. Suggested language: "Pig and Goat had different ideas about hot air balloon travel. Pig thought it was a good idea. Goat, though, did not think it was safe."

4. Work with children to list other parts of the story that are the same and that are different. Record children's ideas in a T-Map like the one shown here.

> **MINILESSON PRINCIPLE**
>
> Think about how the things in a story are the same and how they are different.

Same	Different

SUMMARIZE AND APPLY Restate the minilesson principle. Then tell children to apply it to their independent reading. Suggested language: "When you read, think about how things in the story are the same and how they are different. Look for clues that the author gives you to see how two things are the same or how they are different."

GROUP SHARE Have children name two characters or places from a story they read independently. Ask them to tell one way those things were the same. Then have them tell one way they were different.

▶ The Rainy Trip

INTERACTIVE READ-ALOUD/SHARED READING

Read aloud the story to children. Stop periodically for brief discussion of the story. Use the following suggested stopping points and prompts:

- After Kyra's dad takes everyone to the museum and dinner, ask: "What was the group supposed to be doing on the trip? Why can't they follow their plan?"
- After Ellie and Kyra learn the new game, ask: "What is the problem between Kyra and Ellie?" Follow-up: "How is their problem solved?"
- At the end of the story, say: "The writer was trying to teach you a lesson with this story. What is the lesson? Turn and talk about your ideas with a partner."

MINILESSON Compare and Contrast

TEACH Display the minilesson principle on chart paper, and read it aloud to children. Tell children they are going to learn to notice what is the same and different from the beginning of a story to the end.

1. Remind children that a story has a beginning, a middle, and an end. Explain that a story can be exciting because of the way things change from the beginning to the end. Suggested language: "In the story *The Rainy Trip,* what happened at the beginning?" *(Kyra's family and her friend were on a camping trip. The trip was not fun because it kept raining.)*

> **MINILESSON PRINCIPLE**
> Think about what is the same and what is different from the beginning of a story to the end.

2. Point out to children that looking at how the beginning and end of a story are the same and different helps them better understand the important parts of the story. Suggested language: "At the beginning and end of the story, some things were the same and some things were different. One thing that was the same was that the group was still on the camping trip. One thing that was different was that Ellie and Kyra learned how to have fun."

3. Work with children to identify other things that are the same and different from the beginning to the end of the story. Write their ideas in a T-Map with the labels *Same* and *Different.*

SUMMARIZE AND APPLY Restate the minilesson principle. Tell children to apply it to their independent reading. Suggested language: "When you read, think about what is the same and different from the beginning of the story to the end."

GROUP SHARE Have children explain one way a story they read was the same at the beginning and the end. Then have them explain one way the story was different.

▶ Lewis and Clark's Big Trip

INTERACTIVE READ-ALOUD/SHARED READING

Read aloud the book to children. Stop periodically for brief discussion. Use the following suggested stopping points and prompts:

- After the first page, ask: "Who were Lewis and Clark? What did they do?"
- At the end, say: "Suppose that you took the same trip today that Lewis and Clark took long ago. How would your trip be like theirs? How would it be different? Turn and talk about your ideas with a partner."

MINILESSON Genre: Informational Text

TEACH Explain to children that *Lewis and Clark's Big Trip* is different from the other two stories they read this week because it gives facts and the other stories are made-up. Information books tell about real people, places, and events.

1. Focus on the map to introduce how maps show information. Suggested language: "The story *Lewis and Clark's Big Trip* included a map. A map is a picture that shows where things are and what is near and far away. The title at the top tells that the map shows Lewis and Clark's path across the United States. The key in the bottom left corner explains all of the shapes and colors on the map."

> **MINILESSON PRINCIPLE**
> Think about how maps show information.

2. Write the minilesson principle on chart paper. Work with children to use the features on the map in *Lewis and Clark's Big Trip.* Guide children to find its features, such as rivers and cities. Help them use the key to see what the different shapes and colors on the map stand for. Explain to children that paying attention to maps will help them understand what they read.

SUMMARIZE AND APPLY Restate the minilesson principle. Tell children to apply it to their independent reading. Suggested language: "When you read, look for and use maps to better understand the information you read."

GROUP SHARE Ask children to share examples of maps they have seen in their independent reading. Have them explain the information shown on the map.

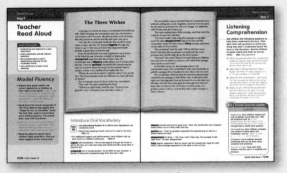

Where Does Food Come From?
Student Book, Lesson 18

The Three Wishes
Teacher's Edition, Lesson 18

Jack and the Beanstalk
Student Book, Lesson 18

▶ Where Does Food Come From?

INTERACTIVE READ-ALOUD/SHARED READING

Read aloud the book to children. Stop periodically for very brief discussion of it. Use the following suggested stopping points and prompts for quick group response, or give a specific prompt and have partners or threes turn and talk.

- After reading about potatoes, ask: "What kind of food are potatoes? Where do they grow?"
- After reading about wheat, ask: "What is wheat? How is it used to make bread?"
- After reading about eggs, ask: "How are milk and eggs the same? How are they different? Turn and talk about your ideas with a partner."
- At the end of the book, ask: "What did you learn about where foods come from?" Follow-up: "What is your favorite food? Where does it come from? How could you find out?"

MINILESSON Author's Purpose

TEACH Display the minilesson principle on chart paper, and read it aloud to children. Tell children they are going to think about why the author wrote the book. Explain that story clues will help them figure that out.

1. Discuss the principle with children, using examples from *Where Does Food Come From?* Suggested language: "In *Where Does Food Come From?*, what did the author write about?" (*The author wrote about where food comes from.*) "How did the author organize the information?" (*The information is organized by the kind of food.*)

> **MINILESSON PRINCIPLE**
>
> Think about why the author wrote the book and what you might learn.

2. Focus on milk. Suggested language: "What did the author tell about milk?" (*The author told where milk comes from and how it is used to make other foods.*) "Why do you think the author told that information?" (*Possible answer: The author wanted to teach that milk comes from cows and that many foods come from milk.*)

3. Use children's responses to explain that authors write for a reason. Suggested language: "An author can write for different reasons. Sometimes it is to teach about a topic. Sometimes it is to tell an entertaining story. In this book, the author gives a lot of information. This gives you a clue that the author wrote to teach you about a topic."

4. Work with children to identify other clues that support the idea that the author wrote the book to teach about a topic. Record children's ideas in an Inference Map like the one shown here.

The author wrote to teach.

SUMMARIZE AND APPLY Restate the minilesson principle. Then tell children to apply it to their independent reading. Suggested language: "When you read, think about why the author wrote the book."

GROUP SHARE Have children identify the reason the author wrote a book they have read. Then have them tell the clues they used to identify that reason.

▶ The Three Wishes

INTERACTIVE READ-ALOUD/SHARED READING

Read aloud the story to children. Stop periodically for brief discussion. Use the following suggested stopping points and prompts:

- After the tree speaks for the first time, ask: "Why does the tree ask the woodcutter not to cut it down? How does the tree reward the woodcutter for saving it?"
- After the sausage falls on the plate, ask: "Do you think that the woodcutter uses his three wishes well? Why or why not?"
- At the end of the story, ask: "What lessons do you think the woodcutter learns? Do you think he will act differently in the future? Turn and talk about your ideas with a partner."

MINILESSON Genre: Fairy Tale

TEACH Display the minilesson principle on chart paper, and read it aloud to children. Tell children they are going to learn to notice that characters in fairy tales can do amazing things. They will also learn to recognize how those things can help or hurt the characters.

1. Remind children that a fairy tale is a made-up story with a lesson. It has imaginary or unbelievable events. The characters can often do things that real people cannot. Suggested language: "In the fairy tale *The Three Wishes*, the characters did amazing things. What did the tree do that real trees cannot?" (*The tree could talk and grant wishes.*)

> **MINILESSON PRINCIPLE**
>
> Notice that the people in fairy tales can do amazing things that help or hurt them.

2. Point out to children that figuring out the amazing things that happen in a fairy tale can help them understand the story. Suggested language: "One amazing thing that happened in this fairy tale was that the tree could talk. Talking saved the tree from being cut down."

3. Work with children to identify other amazing things that happened in the story and discuss how those things helped or hurt the characters. Write their ideas in a T-Map with the labels *Amazing Thing That Happened* and *How It Hurt or Helped*.

SUMMARIZE AND APPLY Restate the minilesson principle. Tell children to apply it to their independent reading. Suggested language: "When you read, think about the amazing things that a character can do. Think about how those amazing things help or hurt the character."

GROUP SHARE Have children identify an amazing thing a character can do. Then have them identify how that amazing thing helped or hurt the character.

▶ Jack and the Beanstalk

INTERACTIVE READ-ALOUD/SHARED READING

Read aloud the story to children. Stop periodically for brief discussion. Use the following suggested stopping points and prompts:

- After the first page, ask: "What did Jack get when he traded the cow? What does that trade tell you about Jack?"
- After the beanstalk grows, ask: "What amazing things happen in the fairy tale? How does each of those amazing things change the rest of the story? Turn and talk about your ideas with a partner."

MINILESSON Genre: Fairy Tale

TEACH Explain to children that *Jack and the Beanstalk* is like *The Three Wishes* because both stories are fairy tales. Point out that both made-up stories tell about amazing things that happen.

1. Introduce the idea that fairy tales have characters that can be nice or mean. Suggested language: "A character is a person or animal in a story. In a fairy tale, a character might also be a talking object or made-up creature like a tree or a giant. In *Jack and the Beanstalk*, there were many characters. They were Jack, his mother, the man who trades the beans, the goose, the cow, and the giant."

> **MINILESSON PRINCIPLE**
>
> Notice that fairy tales have nice characters and mean characters.

2. Write the minilesson principle on chart paper. Explain that nice characters do kind and helpful things and that mean characters are cruel or unkind. Ask children to decide whether the characters Jack, his mother, the man with the beans, and the giant were nice or mean. Have them use story clues and the pictures to explain their ideas. Explain to children that understanding characters will help them understand what they read.

SUMMARIZE AND APPLY Restate the minilesson principle. Tell children to apply it to their independent reading. Suggested language: "When you read, think about each character. Decide if the character is nice or mean."

GROUP SHARE Ask children to share an example of a character from a story they chose for independent reading. Have them tell whether that character is nice or mean.

Whole-Group Lessons

Tomás Rivera
Student Book, Lesson 19

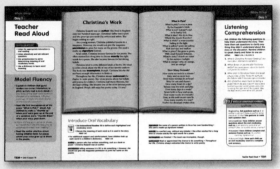

Christina's Work
Teacher's Edition, Lesson 19

Life Then and Now
Student Book, Lesson 19

▶ Tomás Rivera

INTERACTIVE READ-ALOUD/SHARED READING

Read aloud the book to children. Stop periodically for very brief discussion of it. Use the following suggested stopping points and prompts for quick group response, or give a specific prompt and have partners or threes turn and talk.

- After Grandpa takes Tomás to the library, ask: "What do Grandpa and Tomás do together? Why is Grandpa important to Tomás?"
- After Tomás goes to the library, ask: "What do you think will happen to Tomás after he goes to the library? How might the visit to the library change his life?"
- At the end of the story, ask: "How did this book make you feel?" Follow-up: "When have you gone somewhere that changed your life? Turn and talk with a partner about your ideas."

MINILESSON Conclusions

TEACH Display the minilesson principle on chart paper, and read it aloud to children. Tell children they are going to learn how to notice clues about characters as they read. Explain that the clues will help them figure out why characters do things.

1. Discuss the principle with children, using examples of characters from *Tomás Rivera*. Suggested language: "In *Tomás Rivera*, you learned about the events in Tomás Rivera's life. What important event happened to Tomás as a child?" *(His Grandpa took him to the library.)* "What happened when Grandpa took Tomás to the library?" *(Tomás fell in love with stories and books.)*

> **MINILESSON PRINCIPLE**
>
> Think about the characters in a story and why they do things.

2. Focus on Tomás becoming a writer. Suggested language: "Tomás loved his Grandpa's stories. He loved to visit the library. He loved books. What did Tomás do later because of these things?" *(Tomás became a writer.)*

3. Use children's responses to explain how authors give clues about what characters are like and why they do things. Suggested language: "Why did Tomás become a writer? The author did not tell you why exactly, but you can figure it out from the clues in the story. These clues are that Tomás loved stories, books, and the library."

4. Work with children to draw conclusions about other things Tomás does. Record children's ideas in an Inference Map like the one shown here.

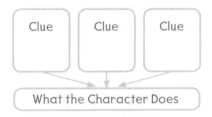

SUMMARIZE AND APPLY Restate the minilesson principle. Explain to children that they can apply it to their independent reading. Suggested language: "When you read a story, think about what the characters do and why. Look for clues that the author tells you about the characters."

GROUP SHARE Have children share a description of a character in a story they chose for independent reading. Ask them to tell what the character did. Then have them give clues from the story that helped them figure out why the character did certain things.

▶ Christina's Work

INTERACTIVE READ-ALOUD/SHARED READING

Read aloud the book to children. Stop periodically for brief discussion. Use the following suggested stopping points and prompts:

- After reading the introduction about Christina, ask: "What words would you use to tell about Christina? What clues in the book tell what she was like?"

- After reading "What Is Pink?," say: "'What Is Pink?' is a poem. How is it the same as other poems you have read? How is it different?"

- At the end of the second page, ask: "How are you and Christina the same? How are you different? Turn and talk with a partner about these ideas."

MINILESSON Conclusions

TEACH Display the minilesson principle on chart paper, and read it aloud to children. Tell children they are going to learn to use what characters say and do to figure out what they are like.

1. Remind children how authors give clues about what characters are like. Explain that clues can be what a person does, says, thinks, and writes. Suggested language: "In *Christina's Work,* the author said that Christina was often sick but kept writing anyway. What does that tell you about Christina?" *(Christina loved to write. Nothing would stop Christina from doing what she loved.)*

> **MINILESSON PRINCIPLE**
>
> Think about how information in a book helps you know what someone is like.

2. Point out to children that information about what people think and do are clues to what they are like. Suggested language: "The author used what Christina thought (she had strong beliefs) and what she did (wrote poems about those beliefs) to show you what Christina was like. You can figure out that Christina was brave and stood up for what she believed in."

3. Work with children to draw additional conclusions from *Christina's Work*. Write their ideas in an Inference Map.

SUMMARIZE AND APPLY Restate the minilesson principle. Explain to children that they should apply it to their independent reading. Suggested language: "When you read, think about what people say, think, and do to figure out what they are like."

GROUP SHARE Have children choose a person they have read about and tell what he or she thought, said, and did. Then have them tell what the person is like.

▶ Life Then and Now

INTERACTIVE READ-ALOUD/SHARED READING

Read aloud the book to children. Stop periodically for brief discussion. Use the following suggested stopping points and prompts:

- After reading the first paragraph, ask: "What does *life then* mean? What words helped you figure it out?"

- At the end of the book, ask: "What might your life have been like if you lived 100 years ago? Turn and talk about your ideas with a partner."

MINILESSON Compare and Contrast

TEACH Explain to children that *Life Then and Now* is both the same as and different from the other two books they read this week. All three books are the same because they are information books. *Life Then and Now,* though, is not a biography. It does not tell about a real person.

1. Focus on types of communication to introduce how authors tell how things are the same and how they are different. Suggested language: "In *Life Then and Now,* the author showed that people used phones in the past and today. The pictures showed that phones have changed. They look different today."

> **MINILESSON PRINCIPLE**
>
> Notice how authors tell how things are the same and how they are different.

2. Page through the book with children to identify a way that things are the same today and in the past. Find a way things are different. Suggested language: "What are things that families did for fun in the past? How is this different from what families do for fun today?" *(In the past, families listened to the radio. Now they watch TV.)*

3. Then write the minilesson principle on chart paper. Guide children to see how the author can use words and pictures to tell how things are the same and how they are different. Explain to children that paying attention to these clues will help them understand what they read.

SUMMARIZE AND APPLY Restate the minilesson principle. Explain to children that they can apply it to their independent reading. Suggested language: "When you read, look for how things are the same and how they are different."

GROUP SHARE Ask children to share an example from their independent reading of things that were the same. Then have them tell about things that were different.

Whole-Group Lessons

Little Rabbit's Tale
Student Book, Lesson 20

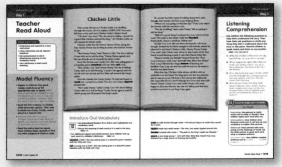

Chicken Little
Teacher's Edition, Lesson 20

Silly Poems
Student Book, Lesson 20

▶ Little Rabbit's Tale

INTERACTIVE READ-ALOUD/SHARED READING

Read aloud the story to children. Stop periodically for very brief discussion of it. Use the following suggested stopping points and prompts for quick group response, or give a specific prompt and have partners or threes turn and talk.

- After Little Rabbit hops off to find Goose, ask: "Why does Little Rabbit think the sky is falling?"
- After Little Rabbit and his friends start off to see Little Rabbit's mother, ask: "Which friends does Little Rabbit tell that the sky is falling? What do they think when he tells them the news?"
- After Little Rabbit and his friends have the meal together, ask: "How did Little Rabbit's friends feel when they found out that the sky was not falling?"
- At the end of the story, ask: "What lesson can you learn from this story?" Follow-up: "When have you made a mistake? What did you learn from it? Turn and talk with a partner about what happened."

MINILESSON Cause and Effect

TEACH Display the minilesson principle on chart paper, and read it aloud to children. Tell children that they are going to learn to notice how one thing happens in a story and then makes other things happen. Explain that word clues and pictures in a story will help them figure out how one thing makes other things happen.

1. Discuss the principle with children, using examples from *Little Rabbit's Tale*. Suggested language: "In the story *Little Rabbit's Tale*, things happened that made other things happen. What happened with the wind while Little Rabbit was sleeping under the tree?" *(The wind blew.)* "What happened because the wind blew?" *(An apple fell from the tree and hit Little Rabbit.)*

> **MINILESSON PRINCIPLE**
>
> Think about how one thing happens and makes other things happen.

2. Focus on what happened after the apple hit Little Rabbit. Suggested language: "One thing that happened was that the apple hit Little Rabbit. That made other things happen. What happened after the apple hit Little Rabbit?" *(Little Rabbit thought the sky was falling and ran off to tell his friends.)*

3. Use children's responses to explain how authors give clues about how one thing in a story makes other things happen. Suggested language: "Right after the apple hit Little Rabbit, he said *The sky is falling. I've got to try to tell everyone*. The picture showed Little Rabbit hopping off to tell his friends. These clues showed that the falling apple made Little Rabbit find his friends."

4. Work with children to name one thing in the story that made other things happen. Record children's ideas in a T-Map like the one shown here.

What Happened	Why It Happened
An apple fell and hit Little Rabbit.	The wind blew.

SUMMARIZE AND APPLY Restate the minilesson principle. Explain to children that they can apply it to their independent reading. Suggested language: "When you read a story, think about how one thing that happens makes other things happen."

GROUP SHARE Have children share one thing that happened in a story they read. Ask them to tell how that thing made other things happen.

▶ Chicken Little

INTERACTIVE READ-ALOUD/SHARED READING

Read aloud the story to children. Stop periodically for brief discussion. Use the following suggested stopping points and prompts:

- After the acorn falls on Chicken Little's head, ask: "Why did Chicken Little think the sky was falling?"
- After Chicken Little and the other friends meet Foxy Loxy, ask: "What plan did Foxy Loxy have for Chicken Little and the other friends? Why did Foxy Loxy have that plan?"
- At the end of the story, ask: "What lesson did Chicken Little learn? Turn and talk with a partner about whether you think it is a good lesson."

MINILESSON Genre: Folktale

TEACH Display the minilesson principle on chart paper, and read it aloud to children. Tell children they are going to learn how to think about how different characters can tell the same story.

1. Remind children that many parts of the stories *Little Rabbit's Tale* and *Chicken Little* are the same. Suggested language: "How are the stories *Little Rabbit's Tale* and *Chicken Little* the same?" *(Something fell on the main character's head. The character in each story thought the sky was falling and went off to tell others.)*

> **MINILESSON PRINCIPLE**
>
> Think about how different characters can tell the same story.

2. Point out that the stories are not exactly the same. Suggested language: "The story *Little Rabbit's Tale* is not exactly the same as *Chicken Little*. The characters are different. Some details are different, too. Little Rabbit went off to tell his friends that the sky was falling. Chicken Little went to tell the king."

3. Work with children to review the setting, characters, and events from *Little Rabbit's Tale* and *Chicken Little*. Write their ideas in separate Story Maps. Use the Story Maps to help children think about how characters can tell the same story. Point out that the stories are usually a little bit different.

SUMMARIZE AND APPLY Restate the minilesson principle. Explain to children that they should apply it to their independent reading. Suggested language: "When you read, think about how different characters can tell the same story. Think about how the stories are the same and how they are different."

GROUP SHARE Have children choose an example of characters that tell the same story. Then have them tell about how the different characters tell the same story.

▶ Silly Poems

INTERACTIVE READ-ALOUD/SHARED READING

Read aloud the introduction and poems to children. Stop periodically for brief discussion. Use the following suggested stopping points and prompts:

- After reading the first page, point out that the picture on the page shows the readers dressed as rabbits. Then say: "Look at the underlined word *hoppy*. Why is the word underlined? What word does Reader 2 mean to use here?" Follow-up: "Why is it funny to say *hoppy* instead of *happy*?"
- After reading the poem "Funny Bunny," ask: "What is the title of this poem? What is special about the two words in the title?" Follow-up: "What other rhyming words can you find in the poem?"

MINILESSON Genre: Poetry

TEACH Explain to children that poetry is a special kind of writing. Tell them that poems may have lines that are the same length and that they often have words that rhyme.

1. Focus on the Langston Hughes poem about the elephant and the mouse to introduce how poems can have silly ideas. Suggested language: "In the poem about the elephant and the mouse, the poet writes that the elephant is afraid of a mouse. This idea sounds silly because an elephant is so big and a mouse is so small."

> **MINILESSON PRINCIPLE**
>
> Notice the silly words and ideas in poems.

2. Page through the poems with children to identify silly words and ideas. Then write the minilesson principle on chart paper. Guide children to see how the author can use silly words and ideas to make the poem more fun to read. Explain to children that paying attention to silly words and ideas will help them understand and enjoy the poems they read.

SUMMARIZE AND APPLY Restate the minilesson principle. Explain to children that they can apply it to their independent reading. Suggested language: "When you read poems, look for silly words and ideas."

GROUP SHARE Ask children to share an example of a poem they read. Then have them identify some of the silly words and ideas in the poem.

Whole-Group Lessons

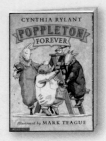

The Tree
Student Book, Lesson 21

Grandpa's Tree
Teacher's Edition, Lesson 21

It Comes from Trees
Student Book, Lesson 21

▶ The Tree

INTERACTIVE READ-ALOUD/SHARED READING

Read aloud the story to children. Stop periodically for very brief discussion of the story. Use the following suggested stopping points and prompts for quick group response, or give a specific prompt and have partners or threes turn and talk.

- After Poppleton calls the tree doctor, ask: "What do you think is wrong with Poppleton's tree?"
- After Cherry Sue suggests a bird feeder, say: "How is Cherry Sue's idea different from the other ideas? Do you think a bird feeder will help the tree?"
- At the end of the story, say: "Think about what Cherry Sue said and did. What kind of character is she? Turn and talk about your ideas with a partner."

MINILESSON Story Structure

TEACH Display the minilesson principle on chart paper, and read it aloud to children. Tell children they are going to learn how to think about the problem in a story and how the characters try to solve it.

1. Discuss the principle with children, using examples from *The Tree*. Suggested language: "In the story *The Tree,* you learned about a problem at the beginning of the story. What problem did Poppleton have?" *(Something was wrong with his tree.)*

2. Focus on Poppleton's first attempt to solve his problem. Suggested language: "Poppleton called a tree doctor, but the tree doctor could not solve the problem. Why couldn't the tree doctor solve the problem?" *(He said the tree was not sick. It needed something.)*

3. Explain that characters may try several different things to solve a problem. Suggested language: "When the tree doctor could not help Poppleton, what did Poppleton do?" *(He asked Hudson what he thought the tree needed.)*

4. Help children tell what Poppleton tried to do to solve his problem. Record their ideas in a Story Map like the one shown here. List attempts at solving the problem under *Middle* and how the problem was solved under *End*.

> **MINILESSON PRINCIPLE**
>
> Notice the problem in the story and how the characters solve it.

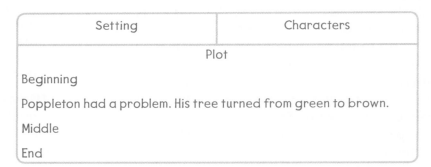

Setting	Characters
Plot	
Beginning	
Poppleton had a problem. His tree turned from green to brown.	
Middle	
End	

SUMMARIZE AND APPLY Restate the minilesson principle. Then tell children to apply it to their independent reading. Suggested language: "When you read a story, think about the problem the character has. Look for different things the character does to try to solve the problem and how the problem is solved."

GROUP SHARE Have children share the problem in a story they chose for independent reading. Ask them to tell what the character did to try to solve the problem. Then have them tell how the problem was solved.

▶ Grandpa's Tree

INTERACTIVE READ-ALOUD/SHARED READING

Read aloud the story to children. Stop periodically for brief discussion. Use the following suggested stopping points and prompts:

- After the first paragraph, ask: "Why is Grandpa's tree special?"
- After Tara suggests that they make a bird feeder, ask: "Why does Grandpa frown when Tara says they should make a bird feeder for the robin?"
- At the end of the story, say: "How did making a bird feeder help Grandpa? Turn and talk about your ideas with a partner."

MINILESSON Story Structure

TEACH Display the minilesson principle on chart paper, and read it aloud to children. Tell children they are going to learn how to look for ways characters work together to solve a problem in a story.

1. Remind children that most stories have a problem that the characters try to solve. Explain that a problem can affect many characters. Suggested language: "In the story *Grandpa's Tree,* Grandpa was grumpy because he broke his leg. How was this also a problem for Tara and Justin?" *(They were sad because they missed doing things with Grandpa.)*

> **MINILESSON PRINCIPLE**
>
> Notice how characters work together to solve a problem.

2. Point out to children that characters often have to work together to solve a problem. Suggested language: "Why did Tara and Justin think a project would solve Grandpa's problem?" *(Grandpa would have something to do.)* Follow-up: "How did finding a project for Grandpa also help Tara and Justin?" *(They were happy because they were doing a project with Grandpa.)*

3. Guide children to complete a Story Map for *Grandpa's Tree.* Help children tell how Tara, Justin, and Dad work together to solve the problem.

SUMMARIZE AND APPLY Restate the minilesson principle. Tell children to apply it to their independent reading. Suggested language: "When you read, think about the problem and how the characters work together to solve it."

GROUP SHARE Have children share the problem in a story they read independently. Then have them tell how the characters in the story work together to solve the problem.

▶ It Comes from Trees

INTERACTIVE READ-ALOUD/SHARED READING

Read aloud the book to children. Stop periodically for brief discussion. Use the following suggested stopping points and prompts:

- After the first paragraph, ask: "How does the author feel about trees? How can you tell?"
- At the end, say: "Think about all the things made from paper and wood. How would life be different if we didn't have trees? Turn and talk about your ideas with a partner."

MINILESSON Genre: Informational Text

TEACH Explain that *It Comes from Trees* is different from the other two stories they read this week. Point out that it is an information book. It gives information about real people, places, or things.

1. Talk about the title and the first paragraph to help children identify the topic. Suggested language: "The author wrote the sentence *Trees can be turned into many useful things.* This gave important information because it told what the rest of the book was about."

> **MINILESSON PRINCIPLE**
>
> Think about the important information the author tells about.

2. Write the minilesson principle on chart paper. Guide children to point out other sentences that have important information about the things that come from trees. Suggested language: "What other sentences have important information? Why is this information important?"

3. Help children realize that the pictures and bar graph give more information about the topic. Suggested language: "What information do you learn by looking at the pictures and the bar graph?" *(I learned how much wood it takes to make things.)*

SUMMARIZE AND APPLY Restate the minilesson principle. Tell children to apply it to their independent reading. Suggested language: "When you read an information book, remember to look for important information in the pictures and in the sentences."

GROUP SHARE Ask children to share examples of important information they found in sentences and in the pictures and graphics in a book they chose for independent reading.

Whole-Group Lessons

Amazing Animals
Student Book, Lesson 22

How Bat Learned to Fly
Teacher's Edition, Lesson 22

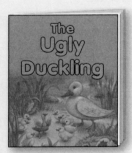

The Ugly Duckling
Student Book, Lesson 22

▶ Amazing Animals

INTERACTIVE READ-ALOUD/SHARED READING

Read aloud the book to children. Stop periodically for very brief discussion of it. Use the following suggested stopping points and prompts for quick group response, or give a specific prompt and have partners or threes turn and talk.

- After reading about the polar bear, ask: "Where is the young polar bear hiding? What clues helped you figure this out?"
- After reading about the camel, ask: "What do the words and pictures tell you about where a camel lives?"
- After reading about the porcupine, say: "How would you describe a porcupine's quills? How do you think other animals learn to stay away from a porcupine's quills?"
- At the end say: "Which animal do you think is the most amazing? Why do you think that? Turn and talk about your ideas with a partner."

MINILESSON Conclusions

TEACH Display the minilesson principle on chart paper, and read it aloud to children. Tell children they are going to learn how to use what they already know to figure out things that the author does not tell them.

1. Discuss the principle with children, using examples from *Amazing Animals.* Suggested language: "A polar bear has thick fur that looks white in the sun. How does what you know about snow and snowy places explain why thick, white fur is important to a polar bear?" *(Snowy places are cold, so thick fur helps keep the polar bear warm. Snow is white, so white fur makes it hard for a polar bear to be seen.)*

> **MINILESSON PRINCIPLE**
>
> Think about what you already know when you read.

2. Focus on what children know about a desert. Suggested language: "What do you know about deserts?" *(A desert is a hot, dry place with sandy soil and few plants.)* "How does this help you understand why the hump on a camel is an important body part?" *(A camel's hump stores fat for food. There is little food in the desert.)*

3. Explain that children can use what they already know to figure things out in a selection. Suggested language: "You learned that ducks use their beaks to eat plants and bugs. What do you think a duck does when it cleans another duck with its beak?" *(It looks for any bugs hiding in the duck's feathers. It eats the bugs it finds.)*

4. Work with children to complete an Inference Map about other animals in the book. Help them understand that they can use the words and pictures along with what they already know to figure out things as they read.

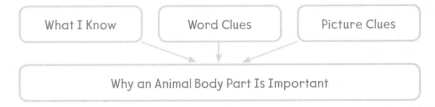

SUMMARIZE AND APPLY Restate the minilesson principle. Then tell children to apply it to their independent reading. Suggested language: "When you read a book, think about what you already know as you read the words and look at the pictures. Use what you already know to help you better understand the book."

GROUP SHARE Have children share an example of something they figured out while reading. Ask them to tell how they used what they already knew along with the words and pictures to figure something out.

▶ How Bat Learned to Fly

INTERACTIVE READ-ALOUD/SHARED READING

Read aloud the story to children. Stop periodically for brief discussion. Use the following suggested stopping points and prompts:

- After learning that Mouse always drops the ball, ask: "What is Mouse's problem?"
- After the first page, ask: "Why does Mouse decide to quit playing ball?"
- After Mother Earth shares her idea: "Will Mother Earth's idea work? Why or why not?"
- At the end of the story, ask: "What does this story explain? Is it like any other stories you have heard or read? Turn and talk about your ideas with a partner."

MINILESSON Conclusions

TEACH Display the minilesson principle on chart paper, and read it aloud to children. Tell children they are going to learn to use what characters do and say to figure out how they feel.

1. Have children recall how at the beginning of *How Bat Learned to Fly*, Mouse was always dropping the ball. Suggested language: "What did Coyote say when Mouse kept dropping the ball?" *(Coyote scolded Mouse. He said,* Why do you always drop the ball when you run?*)*

> **MINILESSON PRINCIPLE**
>
> Think about how the characters feel and the clues that help you know.

2. Point out to children that what characters say and do are clues to how they feel. Suggested language: "The way that Coyote spoke is a clue to how he felt. He scolded Mouse. I know that when someone scolds, they are complaining about something. I can figure out that Coyote was upset and annoyed with Mouse."

3. Help children draw additional conclusions about the way the characters in the story feel. Write their ideas in an Inference Map.

SUMMARIZE AND APPLY Restate the minilesson principle. Tell children to apply it to their independent reading. Suggested language: "When you read, think about how the characters feel and the clues that help you know."

GROUP SHARE Have children choose a character from a story they read and tell what the character said and did. Then have them tell how these clues helped them figure out how the character felt.

▶ The Ugly Duckling

INTERACTIVE READ-ALOUD/SHARED READING

Read aloud the story to children. Stop periodically for brief discussion. Use the following suggested stopping points and prompts:

- After the first paragraph, ask: "How is the gray duck different from the other ducks?"
- After the gray duck leaves the other ducks, ask: "Why do you think the gray duck leaves the other ducks?"
- At the end, ask: "How are ducks and swans alike? How are they different? Turn and talk about your ideas with a partner."

MINILESSON Genre: Fairy Tale

TEACH Explain to children that *The Ugly Duckling* is a fairy tale. Tell them that a fairy tale is an old story with characters that can do amazing things. A fairy tale often begins with the words *Once upon a time* and ends with the words *happily ever after*.

1. Focus on the first two paragraphs of the story. Suggested language: "In the story *The Ugly Duckling*, you learned that one duckling was different from the others. How was the ugly duckling different?" *(He was the last duckling to hatch. He was big and gray. The other ducks did not want to play with him.)*

> **MINILESSON PRINCIPLE**
>
> Notice how characters change in a story.

2. Point out details in the sentences and pictures that tell how the ugly duckling grew and changed. Then write the minilesson principle on chart paper. Guide children to note that even though the ugly duckling was the last to hatch, the pictures show that he grew faster than the other ducklings. Help them realize that the last picture shows the ugly duckling grown up. Ask children to tell how the ugly duckling's feelings changed. Suggested language: "How did the ugly duckling's feelings change once he learned he was a swan?" *(He felt proud and beautiful.)*

SUMMARIZE AND APPLY Restate the minilesson principle. Tell children to apply it to their independent reading. Suggested language: "When you read a story, look for clues that tell how the characters change from the beginning of the story to the end."

GROUP SHARE Ask children to share how another character from a story changed. Have them tell what the character was like at the beginning of the story and what the character was like at the end of the story.

Whole-Group Lessons

▶ Whistle for Willie

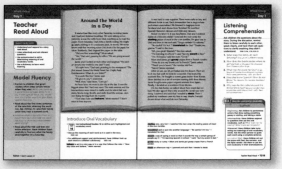

Whistle for Willie
Student Book, Lesson 23

Around the World in a Day
Teacher's Edition, Lesson 23

Pet Poems
Student Book, Lesson 23

INTERACTIVE READ-ALOUD/SHARED READING

Read aloud the story to children. Stop periodically for very brief discussion of the story. Use the following suggested stopping points and prompts for quick group response, or give a specific prompt and have partners or threes turn and talk.

- After Peter tries to whistle for the second time, ask: "What problem does Peter have? What do you think Peter should do to learn how to whistle?"
- After Peter puts on his father's hat, ask: "Why do you think Peter thought feeling grown-up would help him whistle?"
- At the end of the story, say: "How does being able to whistle make Peter feel? Why do you think he keeps whistling? Turn and talk about your ideas with a partner."

MINILESSON Cause and Effect

TEACH Display the minilesson principle on chart paper, and read it aloud to children. Tell children they are going to learn to think about how one thing in a story makes another thing happen.

1. Discuss the principle with children, using examples from *Whistle for Willie*. Suggested language: "In the story *Whistle for Willie*, one thing that Peter did was spin around and around. What happened when Peter stopping spinning?" *(Everything turned down and up and up and down.)* "Why did everything seem to keep moving?" *(Peter was dizzy from spinning. That's the way things look when you are dizzy.)*

> **MINILESSON PRINCIPLE**
>
> Notice when one thing in a story makes another thing happen.

2. Focus on the event to help children see how the first event causes the second event to happen. Suggested language: "What happens when you spin around and then stop spinning?" *(Things seem to keep moving. It's hard to stand up straight.)*

3. Tell children that when they read, they should think about what happens in a story and why. Suggested language: "What happened when Peter hid in the carton and whistled?" *(Willie stopped and looked around.)* "What happened when Peter said, *It's me,* and stood up?" *(Willie raced straight to him.)*

4. Help children identify other events in the story. Record their ideas in a Flow Chart like the one shown here. List the first thing that happens in the first box and then list what it made happen in the second box.

SUMMARIZE AND APPLY Restate the minilesson principle. Then tell children to apply it to their independent reading. Suggested language: "When you read a story, think about what happens in the story. Look for things that make other things happen."

GROUP SHARE Have children choose a story event from their independent reading to share. Have them tell how this thing made another thing in the story happen.

▶ Around the World in a Day

INTERACTIVE READ-ALOUD/SHARED READING

Read aloud the story to children. Stop periodically for brief discussion. Use the following suggested stopping points and prompts:

- After Dad shares the information about the street fair, ask: "What kinds of things do you think happen at a street fair? Do you think a street fair sounds like fun?"
- After the description of the performers, ask: "Which performer would you most like to see? Why?"
- At the end of the story, say: "Do you think the family will go to the street fair next year? Why or why not? Turn and talk about your ideas with a partner."

MINILESSON Genre: Realistic Fiction

TEACH Display the minilesson principle on chart paper, and read it aloud to children. Tell children they are going to learn how thinking about where a story takes place can help them picture what happens.

> **MINILESSON PRINCIPLE**
>
> Think about where a story takes place to help you picture what happens.

1. Remind children that some stories tell about people, places, and things that happen that could be true. Suggested language: "In the story *Around the World in a Day*, where did the family go?" *(They went to an Around the World Street Fair.)*

2. Point out to children that thinking about where a story takes place can help them picture what happens in a story. Suggested language: "This street fair had food, crafts, and souvenirs from many different countries. How did this help you picture what the family did at the street fair?" *(Sample answer: I pictured the family buying food at different stands and eating their food as they walked along.)*

3. Work with children to complete a Web that describes the setting of the story. Help children tell how they pictured the family enjoying the different places in the setting.

SUMMARIZE AND APPLY Restate the minilesson principle. Tell children to apply it to their independent reading. Suggested language: "When you read, think about where a story takes place. Try to picture what happens in the story."

GROUP SHARE Have children share where a story they read takes place. Then have them tell how knowing where the story took place helped them picture one thing that happened.

▶ Pet Poems

INTERACTIVE READ-ALOUD/SHARED READING

Read aloud the introduction and poems to children. Stop periodically for brief discussion. Use the following suggested stopping points and prompts:

- After reading "Bingo," ask: "Who knows this poem as a song?" Invite children who know the song to sing it with you.
- After reading "Little White Horse," ask: "What do you like most about this poem?"
- At the end of "Pet Snake," ask: "Does this poem make you want a pet snake? Why or why not? Turn and talk about your ideas with a partner."

MINILESSON Genre: Poetry

TEACH Explain that poems use words to show things and feelings in different ways. Point out that many poems rhyme, or have words with the same ending sound. Tell children they are going to learn to notice the rhyming words in a poem.

> **MINILESSON PRINCIPLE**
>
> Notice the rhyming words in a poem.

1. Have children focus on the Spanish and English versions of "Little White Horse." Suggested language: "Listen for rhyming words as I read these poems again. What rhyming words did you hear?" *(blanco/reblanco, aquí/nací, snow/go, sea/be)*

2. Review the other two poems with children. Then write the minilesson principle on chart paper. Work with children to identify the rhyming words in "Bingo" and "Pet Snake." Explain to children that rhyming words help make poems fun to read and listen to.

SUMMARIZE AND APPLY Restate the minilesson principle. Tell children to apply it to their independent reading. Suggested language: "When you read a poem, remember to look for rhyming words. Think about how the rhyming words make the poem more interesting to read."

GROUP SHARE Ask children to share examples of rhyming words they found in poems they read for independent reading.

A Butterfly Grows
Student Book, Lesson 24

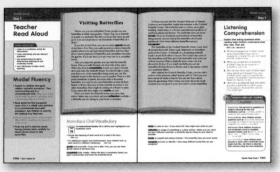

Visiting Butterflies
Teacher's Edition, Lesson 24

Best Friends
Student Book, Lesson 24

▶ A Butterfly Grows

INTERACTIVE READ-ALOUD/SHARED READING

Read aloud the book to children. Stop periodically for very brief discussion of it. Use the following suggested stopping points and prompts for quick group response, or give a specific prompt and have partners or threes turn and talk.

- After reading that the caterpillar eats a leaf for lunch, ask: "What does a caterpillar need to live? How is this like what you need to live? How is it different?"
- After reading that the caterpillar will soon shed its skin, ask: "What do you think happens to a caterpillar when it sheds its skin?"
- At the end, say: "How are a caterpillar and a butterfly the same? How are they different? Turn and talk about your ideas with a partner."

MINILESSON Sequence of Events

TEACH Display the minilesson principle on chart paper, and read it aloud to children. Tell children they are going to learn how to use the information an author gives to figure out how things grow and change.

1. Discuss the principle with children, using examples from *A Butterfly Grows*. Suggested language: "In *A Butterfly Grows*, the author wrote as if the caterpillar was telling the story. What information told how the caterpillar had changed so far?" *(The caterpillar grew in an egg. When it was ready, it hatched.)*

> **MINILESSON PRINCIPLE**
>
> Notice how the author gives information to show how things grow and change.

2. Explain to children that they can think about the order in which things happened to tell how the caterpillar changed. Suggested language: "What happened first in the life of this caterpillar?" *(It grew in an egg.)* "What happened next?" *(It hatched into a tiny caterpillar.)*

3. Point out to children that words such as *first, next, then,* and *last* help tell the order of when things happen. Suggested language: "How can you use the words *first* and *next* to tell how the caterpillar changed?" *(First, the butterfly grew in an egg. Next, it hatched into a caterpillar.)*

4. Work with children to sequence in a Flow Chart the important events in the life of a butterfly. Tell children that understanding the order in which things happen can help them better understand a book.

| First the butterfly grew in an egg | → | Next it hatched into a caterpillar | → | Then | → | Last |

SUMMARIZE AND APPLY Restate the minilesson principle. Then tell children to apply it to their independent reading. Suggested language: "When you read a book, look for information that tells how things grow and change. Put the things that happen in order to help you better understand what is happening."

GROUP SHARE Have children share a few events from a book they have read. Ask them to tell how the information helped them notice how things grew or changed. Encourage children to use the words *first, next, then,* and *last* to describe the order.

▶ Visiting Butterflies

Read aloud the book to children. Stop periodically for brief discussion. Use the following suggested stopping points and prompts:

- After leaving the butterfly house at the Bronx Zoo, say: "Think about seeing animals at a zoo. How is seeing butterflies at a zoo different than seeing other animals at a zoo?"
- At the end of the story, say: "How is visiting butterflies at the Bronx Zoo like visiting butterflies at the Houston Museum of Natural Science? How is it different? Turn and talk about your ideas with a partner."

MINILESSON Sequence of Events

TEACH Display the minilesson principle on chart paper, and read it aloud to children. Tell children they are going to learn to tell what happens first, next, and last in a selection.

1. Remind children that things often happen in a certain order. Suggested language: "In *Visiting Butterflies,* what did you learn you do before you go into the butterfly house?" *(You walk around an outside garden to learn about butterflies and how they grow.)*

> **MINILESSON PRINCIPLE**
>
> Notice what happens first, next, and last when you read.

2. Point out to children that clue words can help tell the order in which things happen. Suggested language: "What do you do after you enjoy the outdoor garden?" *(You walk through one door of the butterfly house into a small space.)*

3. Work with children to use a Flow Chart to sequence the events for visiting butterflies at the Bronx Zoo. Help them tell what happens first, next, and last. Repeat the activity for visiting butterflies at the Houston Museum of Natural Science.

SUMMARIZE AND APPLY Restate the minilesson principle. Tell children to apply it to their independent reading. Suggested language: "When you read, think about the order in which things happen. Think about what happens first, next, and last."

GROUP SHARE Have children tell what happened first, next, and last in a book they have read.

▶ Best Friends

Read aloud the play to children. Stop periodically for brief discussion. Use the following suggested stopping points and prompts:

- After Bird says it hatches from an egg, ask: "How are Bird and Butterfly alike?"
- After Bird says it eats seeds and insects, ask: "If you were a butterfly, how would you feel about Bird eating seeds and insects? Why?"
- At the end of the selection, ask: "Do you think a bird and a butterfly could be friends in real life? Turn and talk about your ideas with a partner."

MINILESSON Genre: Play

TEACH Display the minilesson principle on chart paper, and read it aloud to children. Explain that the author wrote the story *Best Friends* as a play. Have children tell how the play looks different from other stories they have read. Tell children that in a play the characters' words tell the story.

1. Talk about the format of a play with children. Suggested language: "A play has a title. It also has a cast, or a list of the characters in the play. Who is in the cast of this play?" *(Butterfly, Bird)*

> **MINILESSON PRINCIPLE**
>
> Notice that the characters' words tell the story in a play.

2. Page through the play with children to note other features of a play. Point out that the words that come after the characters' pictures are the words that the characters say. Guide children to see that the characters' words tell the story because they tell what the characters do and how they feel. Help children realize that they should read the words as the characters would say them. This will help them understand how the characters feel.

SUMMARIZE AND APPLY Restate the minilesson principle. Tell children to apply it to their independent reading. Suggested language: "When you read a play, remember that the characters' words tell the story."

GROUP SHARE Ask children to share examples of characters' words in a play they have read. Then have children tell how the characters' words told the story.

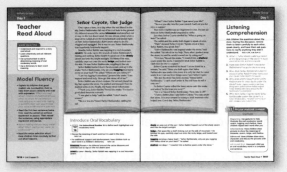

The New Friend
Student Book, Lesson 25

Señor Coyote, the Judge
Teacher's Edition, Lesson 25

Neighborhoods
Student Book, Lesson 25

▶ The New Friend

INTERACTIVE READ-ALOUD/SHARED READING

Read aloud the story to children. Stop periodically for very brief discussion of it. Use the following suggested stopping points and prompts for quick group response, or give a specific prompt and have partners or threes turn and talk.

- After the men begin unloading the moving truck, ask: "Why do you think the boys are so interested in what is happening at the house?"
- After Makoto's parents go to buy food, ask: "How do you think the boys feel about Makoto moving into the house? How might their feelings be different if Makoto was younger or older?"
- At the end of the story, say: "What do you think will happen on Makoto's first day at his new school? Turn and talk about your ideas with a partner."

MINILESSON Understanding Characters

TEACH Display the minilesson principle on chart paper, and read it aloud to children. Remind children that some stories tell about people, places, and things that could be true. Tell children they are going to learn to use the words and pictures in a story to see if the characters act like real people.

1. Discuss the principle with children, using examples from *The New Friend*. Suggested language: "In the story *The New Friend*, a work crew came to wash and paint the empty house. What did the workers bring with them?" *(pails and paint brushes)* "Is this what real workers would bring if they were painting a house?"

2. Draw attention to the picture of the work crew. Suggested language: "Look at the men painting the house. What kind of clothes did they wear to paint the house?" *(overalls, T-shirts, caps)* "Are these clothes a real painter might wear?"

3. Tell children that when they read, they should think about what the characters look like and what they do to decide if they act like real people. Suggested language: "Think about the words and the pictures in the story. What did the boys look like? What were some things that the boys did that were like real boys their age? Did they do anything that a real boy could not do?"

4. Help children record their ideas on a T-Map. Guide them to list what the characters look like and what they do that are like real people.

> **MINILESSON PRINCIPLE**
>
> Notice that characters in some stories look and act like real people.

What the Boys Looked Like	What the Boys Did

SUMMARIZE AND APPLY Restate the minilesson principle. Then tell children to apply it to their independent reading. Suggested language: "When you read a story, think about what the characters look like and what the characters do. Decide if the characters act like real people or if they are make-believe."

GROUP SHARE Have children choose a character from a story to share. Have them describe the character. Then ask children to tell if their character acted like a real person.

▶ Señor Coyote, the Judge

INTERACTIVE READ-ALOUD/SHARED READING

Read aloud the story to children. Stop periodically for brief discussion. Use the following suggested stopping points and prompts:

- After Señor Rattlesnake tells Señor Rabbit to get the stone off of him, ask: "Does this story tell about make-believe characters or real characters? How do you know?"
- After the snake says that a good deed deserves a reward, ask: "Why do you think Señor Rabbit helped the snake? Should people expect a reward for helping others?"
- At the end of the story, say: "Do you think Señor Rattlesnake will learn his lesson? Why or why not? Turn and talk about your ideas with a partner."

MINILESSON Understanding Characters

TEACH Display the minilesson principle on chart paper, and read it aloud to children. Tell children they are going to learn to think about what characters do to better understand the characters.

1. Recall the character Señor Rattlesnake with children. Explain that the way a character behaves can help them better understand the character. Suggested language: "In the story *Señor Coyote, the Judge*, how did Señor Rattlesnake act after Señor Rabbit helped him?" *(He said he wanted to reward Señor Rabbit, but he really planned to eat him.)*

MINILESSON PRINCIPLE

Think about what characters do.

2. Point out to children that thinking about what a character does helps them figure out what the character is like. Suggested language: "The way that Señor Rattlesnake behaved tells me that he is not a nice character and cannot be trusted."

3. Work with children to complete an Inference Map for each character. Record what the character does in the top three boxes. Then record what the character is like in the bottom box.

SUMMARIZE AND APPLY Restate the minilesson principle. Tell children to apply it to their independent reading. Suggested language: "When you read, think about what the story characters do. Use the things that the characters do to decide what the characters are like."

GROUP SHARE Have children share a character from a story they have read and tell what the character did. Then ask children to tell what the character is like based on what he or she did.

▶ Neighborhoods

INTERACTIVE READ-ALOUD/SHARED READING

Read aloud the book to children. Stop periodically for brief discussion. Use the following suggested stopping points and prompts:

- After reading the introduction, ask: "What is special about a neighborhood?"
- At the end, say: "The author tells that people live, work, and go to school in a neighborhood. What else does the author want you to know about neighborhoods? Turn and talk about your ideas with a partner."

MINILESSON Genre: Informational Text

TEACH Explain to children that *Neighborhoods* is different from the other two stories they read this week. It gives information about real places.

1. Point out to children that the title tells what the book is about. Suggested language: "The title, *Neighborhoods*, tells what you will read about. The headings *San Francisco* and *Laredo* tell you where two of the neighborhoods are. What did the author tell you about San Francisco and Laredo?" *(The author told about where the cities are and about festivals that happen in their neighborhoods.)*

MINILESSON PRINCIPLE

Notice how the author shows what things are like.

2. Have children think about the author's words as they look at the pictures and read the captions. Then write the minilesson principle on chart paper. Guide children to point out words that tell what things are like. Suggested language: "Which words help you picture things at the Cherry Blossom Festival?" *(Japanese food, art, music, and dances)* Explain to children that paying attention to words and pictures will help them understand what things are like.

SUMMARIZE AND APPLY Restate the minilesson principle. Tell children to apply it to their independent reading. Suggested language: "When you read about real places, remember to think about how the author shows what they are like."

GROUP SHARE Ask children to name something they read about in a book they chose for independent reading. Have them tell how the author showed what it was like.

Whole-Group Lessons

The Dot
Student Book, Lesson 26

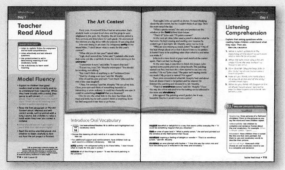

The Art Contest
Teacher's Edition, Lesson 26

Artists Create Art!
Student Book, Lesson 26

▶ The Dot

INTERACTIVE READ-ALOUD/SHARED READING

Read aloud the story to children. Stop periodically for very brief discussion of it. Use the following suggested stopping points and prompts for quick group response, or give a specific prompt and have partners or threes turn and talk.

- After Vashti grabs a marker and jabs the paper, ask: "How does Vashti feel about drawing? How do you know that? Turn and talk about your ideas with a partner."
- After the teacher asks Vashti to sign her paper, ask: "Why does Vashti's teacher ask her to sign the paper?"
- After Vashti sees her dot framed above the teacher's desk, ask: "Why do you think Vashti's teacher framed and hung up her dot?" Follow-up: "What do you think will happen next?"
- At the end of the story, ask: "How do you think the boy felt when Vashti asked him to sign his paper?"

MINILESSON Compare and Contrast

TEACH Display the minilesson principle on chart paper, and read it aloud to children. Tell children they are going to learn how to think about characters as they read.

> **MINILESSON PRINCIPLE**
>
> Notice how characters' feelings are different at the beginning and at the end of a story.

1. Discuss the principle with children, using an example from *The Dot*. Suggested language: "At the beginning of the story *The Dot*, the main character Vashti said that she couldn't draw. How did her feelings toward drawing change by the end of the story?" *(Vashti liked drawing and she even encouraged the boy to draw.)*

2. Focus on when Vashti's teacher asked her to sign the paper. Suggested language: "After Vashti drew her first dot, her teacher said, *Now sign it*. How is this like something that happened later in the story? Do you remember what happened?" *(After the boy said that he couldn't draw a straight line, Vashti asked him to show her. Then she asked him to sign the paper, just like her teacher did.)*

3. Elicit from children additional examples from the story. Prompt them to talk about how Vashti's feelings about trying something new may have changed or how Vashti's teacher's feelings may have changed. Record children's ideas in a T-Map like the one shown here.

Beginning of the Story	End of the Story

SUMMARIZE AND APPLY Restate the minilesson principle. Then tell children to apply it to their independent reading. Suggested language: "When you read, pay attention to the character's feelings. Think about how the character feels differently at the beginning of the story from how he or she feels at the end."

GROUP SHARE Ask children to share what they learned about one character in a story they have read. Have them tell how the character changed from the beginning of the story to the end.

▶ The Art Contest

INTERACTIVE READ-ALOUD/SHARED READING

Read aloud the story to children. Stop periodically for brief discussion. Use the following suggested stopping points and prompts:

- After John exclaims that he can't think of anything to do, ask: "What is the problem in this story?"
- After the line *his mom saved the day*, ask: "How do you think his mom will save the day?"
- At the end of the story, say: "Think about John's new understanding that art doesn't have to be perfect. What do you think the author is trying to tell you? Turn and talk about your ideas with a partner."

MINILESSON Compare and Contrast

TEACH Display the minilesson principle on chart paper, and read it aloud to children. Tell children they are going to learn to think about how characters in different stories are similar.

1. Using the character John from *The Art Contest,* ask children to think about the ways that his feelings changed throughout the story. Suggested language: "In the story *The Art Contest,* we read about John, who didn't like his fire truck painting the year before. By the end of the story, he realized that art doesn't have to be perfect. How do you think he felt about his sunset painting at the end of the story?" *(He was probably proud of his painting. He thought it was beautiful and hoped it would win the art contest.)*

> **MINILESSON PRINCIPLE**
> Think about the ways characters in stories are the same.

2. Talk with children about how Mr. Murphy encourages John to like art. Suggested language: "Mr. Murphy encouraged John to try creating art. How did Mr. Murphy try to encourage John?" *(He told him to close his eyes. He told him that art doesn't have to be perfect.)*

3. Remind children of their discussion about Vashti from *The Dot.* Talk about the ways in which Vashti and John are the same. Point out that the characters' feelings changed in similar ways as well. Write children's ideas in a Venn Diagram.

SUMMARIZE AND APPLY Restate the minilesson principle. Tell children to apply it to their independent reading. Suggested language: "When you read, think about the ways the characters are the same as characters in another story."

GROUP SHARE Ask children to share an example from independent reading of how a character from that story is the same as John or Vashti.

▶ Artists Create Art!

INTERACTIVE READ-ALOUD/SHARED READING

Read aloud the book to children. Stop periodically for brief discussion. Use the following suggested stopping points and prompts:

- After the paragraph about Georges Seurat, say: "The author tells you that you will see many brushstrokes if you look closely at one of Georges Seurat's paintings. How is this different from David Wynne's grizzly bear sculpture?"
- At the end of the story, ask: "How are the three people in this story the same and different? Turn and talk about your ideas with a partner."

MINILESSON Genre: Biography

TEACH Explain to children that *Artists Create Art!* is a biography. Tell them that they are going to learn to notice how the author of a biography tells what is special about the person she is writing about.

1. Introduce the idea that an author writing a biography tells what is special about the person. Suggested language: "In *Artists Create Art!,* the author wrote about three artists. They each created a different kind of art. Their art makes them special."

> **MINILESSON PRINCIPLE**
> Notice how the author tells what is special about the person she is writing about.

2. Ask children to share what else is special about the artists in *Artists Create Art!* Suggested language: "What is special about Grandma Prisbrey?" *(She learned to make art by herself.)* Continue by asking the same question about the other artists.

3. Then guide children to summarize the common features of a biography as you write the minilesson principle on chart paper. Explain to children that knowing what to expect when they read a biography will help them understand what they read.

SUMMARIZE AND APPLY Restate the minilesson principle. Tell children to apply it to their independent reading. Suggested language: "When you read, think about what is special about the person you are reading about."

GROUP SHARE Ask children to explain the things that made a person they read about for independent reading special.

Whole-Group Lessons

What Can You Do?
Student Book, Lesson 27

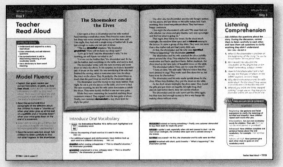

The Shoemaker and the Elves
Teacher's Edition, Lesson 27

The Wind and the Sun
Student Book, Lesson 27

▶ **What Can You Do?**

INTERACTIVE READ-ALOUD/SHARED READING

Read aloud the book to children. Stop periodically for very brief discussion of it. Use the following suggested stopping points and prompts for quick group response, or give a specific prompt and have partners or threes turn and talk.

- After the quote about learning to swim, ask: "Did this girl always know how to swim? How did she become good at it?"
- After the sentence, *We're happy when we do something well*, ask: "How do you feel when you do something well?" Follow-up: "How do you feel when you're learning something new?"
- After the sentences about Marie, Jill, and Gene, ask: "How do you think Marie, Jill, and Gene became good at spelling, printing, and working with computers? Turn and talk about your ideas with a partner."
- At the end, repeat the final question and ask: "What can you do? What would you like to learn how to do?"

MINILESSON Text and Graphic Features

TEACH Display the minilesson principle on chart paper, and read it aloud to children. Tell children they are going to notice how pictures and words go together as they read.

1. Discuss the principle with children, using examples of photographs from *What Can You Do?* Suggested language: "In *What Can You Do?*, there are many photographs. What do these pictures show?" *(These pictures show children doing things they are good at. They also show children learning how to do things.)*

> **MINILESSON PRINCIPLE**
>
> Notice how words and pictures go together in books.

2. Focus on one spread, such as the photographs of parents helping their children. Suggested language: "The words on this page say *When things are hard, we need help to learn.* How do the pictures match these words?" *(The pictures show parents helping their children. The parents will help the children to learn. The pictures match what the words say.)*

3. Use children's responses to explain how words and pictures go together in books. Suggested language: "The pictures in a story usually match the words. The author says the same thing with words that the illustrator or photographer does with pictures."

4. Elicit from children additional examples from the book of ways the words match the pictures. Record children's ideas in a T-Map like the one shown here.

What the Words Say	What the Pictures Show

SUMMARIZE AND APPLY Restate the minilesson principle. Then tell children to apply it to their independent reading. Suggested language: "When you read, think about what the words say and what the pictures show. Think about how the words and pictures go together."

GROUP SHARE Ask children to explain what they learned about how words and pictures go together by sharing a specific pairing from a story they read. Tell them to explain how the words are saying what the pictures are showing.

▶ The Shoemaker and the Elves

INTERACTIVE READ-ALOUD/SHARED READING

Read aloud the story to children. Stop periodically for brief discussion. Use the following suggested stopping points and prompts:

- After the first paragraph, ask: "When and where does this story take place?"
- After the shoemaker's wife suggests that they stay up to find out what is going on, ask: "Why does the shoemaker's wife want to stay up? What do you think will happen next?"
- At the end of the story, say: "Think about how the story ends. What lesson can you learn from this story? Turn and talk about your ideas with a partner."

MINILESSON Genre: Fairy Tale

TEACH Display the minilesson principle on chart paper, and read it aloud to children. Tell children they are going to learn to think about what happens to characters in a story.

1. Using the shoemaker from *The Shoemaker and the Elves,* discuss with children what happened to characters in the story. Suggested language: "In the story *The Shoemaker and the Elves*, the shoemaker had trouble running his shoe store. Something happened that helped the shoemaker. What happened to him?" *(The elves came and made a beautiful pair of shoes for him.)*

> **MINILESSON PRINCIPLE**
>
> Think about what happens to characters in a story.

2. Talk with children about what happened to the elves. Suggested language: "We learned in the story that the shoemaker wanted to thank the elves for their help. What did the shoemaker do to thank the elves?" *(He and his wife made special shoes for the elves.)*

3. Discuss with children what happens to characters in the story. Remind them to think about what happens in order. Fill out a Flow Chart with what happens to the characters in *The Shoemaker and the Elves.*

SUMMARIZE AND APPLY Restate the minilesson principle. Tell children to apply it to their independent reading. Suggested language: "When you read, think about what happens to characters in the story."

GROUP SHARE Ask children to share an example from independent reading of something that happens to a character.

▶ The Wind and the Sun

INTERACTIVE READ-ALOUD/SHARED READING

Read aloud the story to children. Stop periodically for brief discussion. Use the following suggested stopping points and prompts:

- After Wind suggests having a contest, ask: "Why do Sun and Wind decide to have a contest?" Follow-up: "Who do you think will win?"
- After the traveler wraps his jacket tighter, ask: "Did Wind's idea turn out the way he thought it would?" Follow-up: "Why or why not?"
- At the end of the story, ask: "What other stories have we read that are like this one? Turn and talk about your ideas with a partner."

MINILESSON Genre: Fable

TEACH Explain to children that *The Wind and the Sun* is different from the other two stories children read this week. Point out that it is a fable, and that a fable is a story that teaches a lesson.

1. Focus on what the characters do in *The Wind and the Sun* to introduce the idea that fables teach lessons. Suggested language: "In the story *The Wind and the Sun*, Wind and Sun did different things. Wind tried to use force to get Traveler to take off his coat. Sun used warmth, and that worked better. The lesson is that it is better to use kindness instead of force."

> **MINILESSON PRINCIPLE**
>
> Think about what the characters do and how the author is teaching you a lesson.

2. Write the minilesson principle on chart paper. Help children to understand that what the characters do can teach a lesson. Have children retell Wind's and Sun's actions in their own words and connect that to the story's lesson. Explain to children that figuring out what the characters in a story do will help them understand the lesson.

SUMMARIZE AND APPLY Restate the minilesson principle. Tell children to apply it to their independent reading. Suggested language: "When you read, look for a lesson that the author is teaching."

GROUP SHARE Ask children to retell a lesson from a story they read for independent reading. Have them explain how what the characters did helped teach the lesson.

The Kite
Student Book, Lesson 28

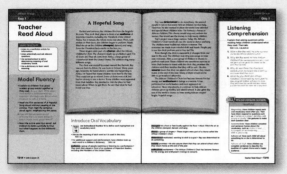

A Hopeful Song
Teacher's Edition, Lesson 28

Measuring Weather
Student Book, Lesson 28

▶ The Kite

INTERACTIVE READ-ALOUD/SHARED READING

Read aloud the story to children. Stop periodically for very brief discussion of it. Use the following suggested stopping points and prompts for quick group response, or give a specific prompt and have partners or threes turn and talk.

- After the robins tell Frog and Toad to give up, ask: "Why did the robins laugh?" Follow-up: "Do you think Frog and Toad will give up? Why or why not?"
- After the kite falls down with a thud, ask: "Which word helps you best picture what happened to the kite? Why?"
- After Toad suggests going home, ask: "How do you think Toad feels? Turn and talk about your ideas with a partner."
- At the end of the story, ask: "What can you learn from this story?"

MINILESSON Story Structure

TEACH Display the minilesson principle on chart paper, and read it aloud to children. Tell children they are going to learn to think about how characters in a story solve a problem.

1. Discuss how characters solve a problem using examples from *The Kite*. Focus on Frog and how he solved the problem of getting the kite to fly. Suggested language: "In order to know how a character solved a problem, we need to know what that problem was. What was the problem in *The Kite*?" *(The kite wouldn't fly.)*

> **MINILESSON PRINCIPLE**
>
> Think about how the characters in a story solve a problem.

2. Use children's responses to talk about how Frog solved the problem. Suggested language: "Frog didn't quit when the kite wouldn't fly. He kept trying different things, like telling Toad to run, jump, wave, and shout."

3. Work with children to complete a Story Map that shows the setting, characters, and plot. Make sure that children recognize the problem and how it is solved.

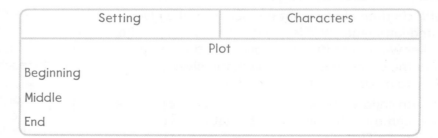

Setting	Characters
Plot	
Beginning	
Middle	
End	

SUMMARIZE AND APPLY Restate the minilesson principle. Then tell children to apply it to their independent reading. Suggested language: "When you read, think about how the characters in a story solve a problem."

GROUP SHARE Ask children to share what the characters did to solve the problem in a story they have read.

▶ A Hopeful Song

INTERACTIVE READ-ALOUD/SHARED READING

Read aloud the book to children. Stop periodically for brief discussion. Use the following suggested stopping points and prompts:

- After the first paragraph, ask: "How does the opening paragraph make you feel?"
- After the third paragraph, ask: "Why did Ray Barnett go to Africa?"
- At the end of the story, say: "Why is the title of this story *A Hopeful Song*? Turn and talk about your ideas with a partner."

MINILESSON Genre: Informational Text

TEACH Display the minilesson principle on chart paper, and read it aloud to children. Tell children they are going to learn to think about how the author feels about what he is writing about.

1. Using the story *A Hopeful Song,* discuss with children that authors show how they feel about a topic through what they write. Suggested language: "Authors write stories for specific reasons. Often, the reason an author writes a book gives us a clue about how he or she feels. Why do you think the author of *A Hopeful Song* wrote this book?" *(to inform people about a choir that he likes very much)*

> **MINILESSON PRINCIPLE**
>
> Think about how the author feels about what he is writing about.

2. Explain to children that an author will include clues to show his or her feelings and reasons for writing. Suggested language: "What words in the story give you clues about how the author feels about the African Children's Choir?" *(The word "successful" makes me think that the author thinks that the African Children's Choir is doing well.)*

3. Discuss with children other clues that tell how an author feels about what he is writing about. Write their ideas in an Inference Map.

SUMMARIZE AND APPLY Restate the minilesson principle. Tell children to apply it to their independent reading. Suggested language: "When you read, look for clues that tell you how the author feels."

GROUP SHARE Ask children to explain how the author of their independent reading book feels. Have them support this idea with clues they have found in the book.

▶ Measuring Weather

INTERACTIVE READ-ALOUD/SHARED READING

Read aloud the book to children. Stop periodically for brief discussion. Use the following suggested stopping points and prompts:

- After the paragraph about the thermometer, ask: "How are a thermometer and a rain gauge the same?" Follow-up: "How are they different?"
- At the end of the story, ask: "How it helpful to know what the temperature is going to be each day? Turn and talk about your ideas with a partner."

MINILESSON Genre: Informational Text

TEACH Write the minilesson principle on chart paper, and read it aloud. Explain to children that *Measuring Weather* is an information book that gives information about a topic. It includes a graph to give more information about the topic.

1. Focus on the graph to introduce how graphs give information. Suggested language: "In *Measuring Weather,* the author included a graph that showed the daily temperature for a week. This type of graph is called a *bar graph.*"

> **MINILESSON PRINCIPLE**
>
> Think about the information in graphs.

2. Ask children to share what they remember about the graph in *Measuring Weather*. Guide children to understand how the information found in a graph is often easier to understand because it uses pictures and words together. Help them recognize the parts of a bar graph that help them understand information, such as headings and bars.

SUMMARIZE AND APPLY Restate the minilesson principle. Tell children to apply it to their independent reading. Suggested language: "When you read a book with graphs, think about the information in graphs."

GROUP SHARE Ask children to explain the information they learned from a graph found in their independent reading.

Whole-Group Lessons

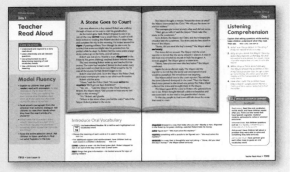

A Boat Disappears
Student Book, Lesson 29

A Stone Goes to Court
Teacher's Edition, Lesson 29

Busy Bugs
Student Book, Lesson 29

▶ A Boat Disappears

INTERACTIVE READ-ALOUD/SHARED READING

Read aloud the story to children. Stop periodically for very brief discussion of it. Use the following suggested stopping points and prompts for quick group response, or give a specific prompt and have partners or threes turn and talk.

- After Skeet said his boat was gone, ask: "What is the problem in this story?"
- After Inspector Hopper says, *Let's follow this trail*, ask: "What do Skeet and Inspector Hopper see?" Follow-up: "Why do they follow the trail of leaf bits?"
- After Inspector Hopper thanks Sally, ask: "Who have Inspector Hopper, McBugg, and Skeet asked about the boat so far?" Follow-up: "What do they each say?"
- At the end of the story, ask: "What happened to Skeet's boat?" Follow-up: "How can Skeet be more careful to protect his boat in the future?"

MINILESSON Cause and Effect

TEACH Display the minilesson principle on chart paper, and read it aloud to children. Tell children they are going to learn to think about what characters do and why.

1. Discuss the principle with children, using examples of characters from *A Boat Disappears*. Suggested language: "In the story *A Boat Disappears*, we got to know a few characters as we read. Who were these characters?" *(Skeet, Inspector Hopper, McBugg, Eensy Weensy, Sally, Conrad)*

2. Focus on one character, such as Skeet. Suggested language: "Why did Skeet go to Inspector Hopper for help?" *(Skeet's boat disappeared, and he wanted Inspector Hopper to help him find it.)*

3. Use children's responses to explain that characters do things for a reason. Suggested language: "There is always something that causes a character to do something. Because Skeet's boat disappeared, he went to see Inspector Hopper."

4. Elicit from children additional examples of cause and effect from the story, such as Conrad helping Skeet find a new boat because he ate his original boat. Record children's ideas in a T-Map like the one shown here.

> **MINILESSON PRINCIPLE**
>
> Think about what characters do and why.

What the Character Does	Why the Character Does It

SUMMARIZE AND APPLY Restate the minilesson principle. Then tell children to apply it to their independent reading. Suggested language: "When you read, think about what the characters do. Then think about the reason why they did what they did."

GROUP SHARE Ask children to share what they learned about one character in their independent reading. Ask them to tell what the character did and why.

▶ A Stone Goes to Court

INTERACTIVE READ-ALOUD/SHARED READING

Read aloud the story to children. Stop periodically for brief discussion. Use the following suggested stopping points and prompts:

- After reading the sentence containing the word *disguised,* ask: "What clues in this sentence would help you understand the word *disguised?*"
- After Robert points to the stone, say: "Think about the title of the story. What do you think will happen next?"
- At the end of the story, say: "Think about the main problem in this story. How was the problem solved? Turn and talk about your ideas with a partner."

MINILESSON Cause and Effect

TEACH Display the minilesson principle on chart paper, and read it aloud to children. Tell children they are going to learn to think about what characters do and why.

1. Using the character of the Mayor from *A Stone Goes to Court,* discuss with children that characters do certain things for a reason. Suggested language: "In the story *A Stone Goes to Court,* we read about a boy named Robert whose money was stolen. The Mayor arrested a stone for the crime. How did the Mayor get the money back?" *(When the townspeople laughed about the stone being charged with a crime, the Mayor fined them for being disrespectful and gave the money to Robert.)*

> **MINILESSON PRINCIPLE**
>
> Think about what characters do and why.

2. Talk with children about the Mayor's reason for doing this. Suggested language: "The Mayor must have had a reason for arresting a stone. Why do you think he did this?" *(He knew he would never find the man in green clothing, so he came up with a plan to get Robert's money back.)*

3. Discuss with children the cause of other characters' actions. Write their ideas in a T-Map labeled *What the Character Does* and *Why.*

SUMMARIZE AND APPLY Restate the minilesson principle. Tell children to apply it to their independent reading. Suggested language: "When you read, think about what characters do and why."

GROUP SHARE Ask children to share an example from independent reading of something a character did and why the character did it.

▶ Busy Bugs

INTERACTIVE READ-ALOUD/SHARED READING

Read aloud the introduction and poems to children. Stop periodically for brief discussion. Use the following suggested stopping points and prompts:

- After the snail poems, say: "The first poem is written in Spanish. The second poem is the English version of the first poem. What do you think the Spanish word for *snail* is?"
- After reading "Song of the Bugs," ask: "What line is repeated in this poem?" Follow-up: "Why did the author repeat the same line twice? Turn and talk about your ideas with a partner."

MINILESSON Genre: Poetry

TEACH Point out that *Busy Bugs* is a collection of poems. Tell children that poets include specific words in their poems to make readers feel a certain way.

1. Focus on "Worm" to introduce the way a poem can make you feel. Suggested language: "In 'Worm,' the poet used many words that rhymed. When you read this poem out loud, the words are fun to say. This can make you feel happy, or it can make you feel nervous if you don't like worms."

> **MINILESSON PRINCIPLE**
>
> Think about how a poem makes you feel.

2. Write the minilesson principle on chart paper. Guide children to think about how the different poems in *Busy Bugs* made them feel. Encourage them to choose specific lines or words that made them feel a certain way. Have children explain the words they chose.

SUMMARIZE AND APPLY Restate the minilesson principle. Tell children to apply it to their independent reading. Suggested language: "When you read, think about how a poem makes you feel."

GROUP SHARE Ask children to explain the feeling they got from a poem they read for independent reading.

Whole-Group Lessons

Winners Never Quit!
Student Book, Lesson 30

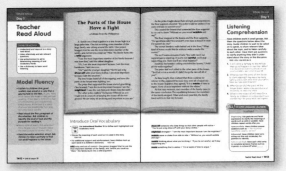

The Parts of the House Have a Fight
Teacher's Edition, Lesson 30

Be a Team Player
Student Book, Lesson 30

▶ Winners Never Quit!

INTERACTIVE READ-ALOUD/SHARED READING

Read aloud the story to children. Stop periodically for very brief discussion of it. Use the following suggested stopping points and prompts for quick group response, or give a specific prompt and have partners or threes turn and talk.

- After Garrett tells Mia, *Better luck next time!*, ask: "How do you think Mia feels when she can't score a goal and no one cheers?" Follow-up: "How is this feeling different from how she feels when she scores a goal and her teammates cheer?"

- After Mia stomps to the house, ask: "Why did the author use the word *stomped*? Turn and talk with your partner about how words can help you make a picture in your mind."

- After Mia stands by the side and watches, ask: "How do you think Mia feels watching everyone else play soccer?" Follow-up: "How do you think she feels now about quitting?"

- At the end of the story, ask: "What lesson did Mia learn?"

MINILESSON Understanding Characters

TEACH Display the minilesson principle on chart paper, and read it aloud to children. Tell children they are going to learn how to notice what characters say and do as they read.

1 Discuss the principle with children, using examples of characters from *Winners Never Quit!* Focus on what Mia said and did to help children understand her. Suggested language: "In the middle of the story, Mia quit. Why did she quit?" *(When Mia scored a goal, everyone cheered. But when she didn't score a goal, no one cheered, so she quit.)*

> **MINILESSON PRINCIPLE**
>
> Notice what characters say and what they do.

2. Use children's responses to explain how what characters say and what they do are clues to understanding that character. Suggested language: "Mia quit because she didn't like to lose. You can tell she didn't like to lose by what she said and did."

3. Elicit from children additional examples from the story. Record children's ideas in a T-Map like the one shown here.

What Mia Said	What Mia Did

SUMMARIZE AND APPLY Restate the minilesson principle. Then tell children to apply it to their independent reading. Suggested language: "When you read, think about what the characters say and do. Think about what you find out about the characters by what they say and do."

GROUP SHARE Ask children to share what they learned about a character they have read about. Tell them to explain what the character said and did that helped them learn about the character.

▶ The Parts of the House Have a Fight

INTERACTIVE READ-ALOUD/SHARED READING

Read aloud the story to children. Stop periodically for brief discussion. Use the following suggested stopping points and prompts:

- After the tree house hears the family fighting, ask: "Do you think this story really happened? Why or why not?"
- At the end of the story, say: "Think about the whole story. How are the family members and the parts of the house the same? Turn and talk about your ideas with a partner."

MINILESSON Genre: Folktale

TEACH Explain to children that *The Parts of the House Have a Fight* is a folktale from the Philippines. Tell children that folktales are stories that were made up many years ago. Folktales are often not real, but they may teach a lesson.

1. Using the story *The Parts of the House Have a Fight,* discuss with children that a folktale includes things which could not actually happen. Suggested language: "In the folktale *The Parts of the House Have a Fight,* you read about a family fighting about who is the most important member. What happened because of their fighting?" *(Their fighting caused the parts of the house to begin arguing over which part was the most important.)*

> **MINILESSON PRINCIPLE**
>
> Think about what a story really means.

2. Talk with children about why the author might have included a similar fight among the family members and among the parts of the house. Suggested language: "The family members have the same argument that the parts of the house have. Why do you think the author made the parts of the house fight, too?" *(to show that the family members are like parts of a house, all different, but all important)*

3. Write the minilesson principle on chart paper. Guide children to understand that an author might not come out and say what a story really means. Help them recognize that they can use clues from the story and what they already know to help them understand what a story really means.

SUMMARIZE AND APPLY Restate the minilesson principle. Tell children to apply it to their independent reading. Suggested language: "When you read, think about what a story really means."

GROUP SHARE Ask children to share an example from independent reading of what they think a story really means.

▶ Be a Team Player

INTERACTIVE READ-ALOUD/SHARED READING

Read aloud the book to children. Stop periodically for brief discussion. Use the following suggested stopping points and prompts:

- After the fourth paragraph, ask: "Why is it important to be a team player?"
- After the checklist, say: "One of the things on this checklist is to follow the rules. Why do you think it is important to follow all, and not just some, of the rules on this checklist? Turn and talk about your ideas with a partner."

MINILESSON Genre: Informational Text

TEACH Explain to children that *Be a Team Player* is different from the other two stories they read this week. Point out that it is an information book. It tells how to do something.

1. Focus on the checklist at the end of the book. Suggested language: "In *Be a Team Player,* the author included a checklist that gives rules about how to be a team player."

> **MINILESSON PRINCIPLE**
>
> Think about the most important information.

2. Write the minilesson principle on chart paper. Then guide children to read back through *Be a Team Player* and to name important information in the book. Suggested language: "Which is more important: *People may play on a field or on a court* or *No matter what kind of team it is, it's important to be a good team player*? Why?" *(The second sentence; it tells about a big idea that is important no matter what you do.)*

SUMMARIZE AND APPLY Restate the minilesson principle. Tell children to apply it to their independent reading. Suggested language: "When you read, think about the most important information."

GROUP SHARE Ask children to explain what the most important information is in a book they read for independent reading and why that is the most important information.

Teacher's Notes

Teaching Genre

Genre instruction and repeated exposure to a variety of genres are essential components of any high-quality literacy program. Access to the tools children need to understand information in different genres will make them better readers. When children understand the characteristics of a variety of genres, they will be able to:

- gain an appreciation for a wide range of texts
- develop a common vocabulary for talking about texts
- begin reading texts with a set of expectations related to genre
- make evidence-based predictions
- develop preferences as readers
- understand purposes for reading and writing
- recognize the choices an author makes when writing
- compare and contrast texts
- think deeply about what they read

The pages in this section provide a framework for discussing genre with your students in an age-appropriate way. You can use the lists on the following pages to organize for genre discussion.

- **Genre Characteristics:** teach and review the salient features
- **Discussion Starters:** begin and maintain productive discussions
- **Comparing Texts:** encourage children to make connections across texts
- **Literature:** select *Journeys* literature for discussion

Fantasy 102

Fairy Tale 104

Folktale 105

Fable 106

Realistic Fiction 107

Informational Text 108

Biography 110

Poetry 111

Fantasy

SUPPORT THINKING

DISCUSSION STARTERS During whole-group and small-group discussion, use questions to spark conversation about genre characteristics.

- Who is this story about?
- What is [character name] like? What can he/she do that is special?
- What is happening in this story?
- What problem does [character name] have?
- Where is this story happening? Is it a place that you would like to visit? Explain.
- Which parts of this story could not happen in real life?
- Which people could not live in the real world? How do you know?
- Would you like to read more stories that are like [title]? Why or why not?

COMPARING TEXTS After children have read and listened to several fantasy stories, prompt them to compare selections and to recognize common characteristics. Use questions such as these:

- How are the people in [title] and [title] alike? How are they different?
- How is [title] the same as other stories you have read? How is it different?
- How is the ending of [title] different from the ending of [title]?

Gus Takes the Train,
Student Book,
Lesson 5

A Cupcake Party,
Student Book,
Lesson 10

Genre Characteristics

A fantasy story is a made-up story that could not happen in real life.

Through repeated exposure to fantasy stories, children should learn to notice common genre characteristics, though at Grade 1 they will not be expected to use the technical labels (except for *characters* and *setting*). Use friendly language to help them understand the following concepts:

- **Author's Purpose:** to entertain
- **Characters:** the people or animals in a story; characters in fantasy stories often have special abilities
- **Characters' Actions/Qualities:** may have both real and make-believe qualities
  - animals and objects may talk and act like people
  - people may have feelings like those of real people but can do amazing things
- **Setting:** where and when the story takes place
  - may be a real place or a make-believe place
  - the story may be set in a different time
- **Plot:** what happens in the story
  - includes a problem at the beginning, things that happen as characters try to solve the problem, and an ending
  - the problem may be similar to problems in real life
  - characters may have realistic or make-believe solutions to problems
- **Dialogue:** the words that characters say to each other
- **Theme/Message:** what the author is trying to say to readers

JOURNEYS Literature

STUDENT BOOK

The Big Race
The Big Trip
A Boat Disappears
A Cupcake Party
Curious George at School
Gus Takes the Train
The Kite
The Tree

TEACHER'S EDITION READ-ALOUD

Chipper Chips In
The Dancing Wolves
Susie and the Bandits

LEVELED READERS

The Barnyard Bandit **K**
Bear Swims **E**

Ben the Cat **D**
The Boat Race **J**
Bobcat Tells a Tale **J**
Cam the Camel **K**
A Cat Named Ben **D**
Chipmunk's New Home **I**
A Chunk of Cheese **F**
Cow's Lunch **I**
Curious George at the Library **I**
Curious George Finds Out
  About School **B**
Curious George Visits School **C**
Curious George's Day at School **C**
Flying **H**
Flying in an Airplane **H**
Forest Stew **H**
Happy Birthday, Toad **E**
Izzy's Move **D**
A Job for Jojo **J**

Lena's Garden **J**
The Map and the Treasure **I**
The Missing Glove **F**
The Mountain **J**
Polar Bear Pete **H**
Polly's Pet Polar Bear **G**
Putting Frosting on the Cake **D**
The Sailboat Race **J**
The Sand Castle **K**
A Seed for Sid **E**
Skunk Cooks Soup **G**
Toad's Birthday **E**
The Treasure Map **I**
Trip to the Rock **B**
Where Is Cow's Lunch? **H**

Fairy Tale

SUPPORT THINKING

DISCUSSION STARTERS During whole-group and small-group discussion, use questions to spark conversation about genre characteristics.

- Who is this story about?
- What happens in this story?
- What problem does [character name] have?
- How do things turn out for people who are good? For people who are bad?
- Where is this story happening?
- Which characters get along? Which characters do not get along?
- Which parts of this story could not happen in real life?
- Which people could not live in the real world? How do you know?
- Which words are clues that this story is a fairy tale?
- Do you like the way the story ended? Why or why not?

COMPARING TEXTS After children have read and listened to several fairy tales, prompt them to compare stories and to recognize common characteristics. Use questions such as these:

- How is [title] the same as other stories you have read?
- How is [character name] like characters in other stories you have read?
- Have you read about any other characters that can do the same things as [character name]?
- Which fairy tale do you like better—[title] or [title]?

 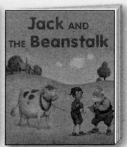

The Three Little Pigs, Student Book, Lesson 6

Jack and the Beanstalk, Student Book, Lesson 18

Genre Characteristics

A fairy tale is a made-up story in which characters can do amazing things. It has been told over and over for many years.

Through repeated exposure to fairy tales, children should learn to notice common genre characteristics, though at Grade 1 they will not be expected to use the technical labels (except for *characters* and *setting*). Use friendly language to help them understand the following concepts:

- **Author's Purpose:** to entertain
- **Characters:** the people or animals in a story; characters in fairy tales often have special powers or can do amazing things; some characters are good and some are bad
- **Setting:** where and when the story takes place; usually set long ago in a faraway place
- **Plot:** what happens in the story; includes a problem at the beginning, things that happen as characters try to solve the problem, and an ending
- **Dialogue:** the words that characters say to each other
- **Storybook Language:** memorable beginning and ending language such as *Once upon a time* and *happily ever after*
- **Transformations:** a change in form of a person or an object
- **Theme/Message:** what the author is trying to say to readers

JOURNEYS Literature

STUDENT BOOK
Jack and the Beanstalk
The Three Little Pigs
The Ugly Duckling

TEACHER'S EDITION READ-ALOUD
The Little Red Hen
The Shoemaker and the Elves
The Three Wishes

Folktale

Genre Characteristics

A folktale is a made-up story that was first told aloud to explain something or to teach a lesson. It has been told over and over for many years.

Through repeated exposure to folktales, children should learn to notice common genre characteristics, though at Grade 1 they will not be expected to use the technical labels (except for *characters* and *setting*). Use friendly language to help them understand the following concepts:

- **Author's Purpose:** to entertain; to teach a lesson
- **Characters:** the people or animals in a story; animals may talk and act like people
- **Setting:** where and when the story takes place; usually set long ago in a specific place (often where the story originated)
- **Plot:** what happens in the story; includes a problem that characters face, things that happen as characters try to solve the problem, and an ending
- **Dialogue:** the words that characters say to each other
- **Theme/Message:** what the author is trying to say to readers
  - often tells what a group of people believes
  - may tell a group's explanation for why things are the way they are

JOURNEYS Literature

STUDENT BOOK
How Leopard Got His Spots
Little Rabbit's Tale

TEACHER'S EDITION READ-ALOUD
Chicken Little
How Bat Learned to Fly

The Neighbors
The Parts of the House
  Have a Fight
Señor Coyote, the Judge
A Stone Goes to Court
Stone Stew
Turtle, Frog, and Rat

LEVELED READERS
Bear's Long, Brown
  Tail **H**
Bear's Tail **H**
Giraffe's Neck **R**
Peacock's Tail **L**

SUPPORT THINKING

DISCUSSION STARTERS During whole-group and small-group discussion, use questions to spark conversation about genre characteristics.

- Who is this story about?
- What is [character name] like?
- What is happening in this story?
- What problem does [character name] have? How does [character name] work out the problem?
- Where is this story happening? What is the place like?
- What can you tell about [character name] by what he/she says?
- Which parts of this story could not happen in real life? Explain how you know.
- What lesson can you learn by reading this story?

COMPARING TEXTS After children have read and listened to several folktales, prompt them to compare stories and to recognize common characteristics. Use questions such as these:

- How are the characters in [title] and [title] the same?
- How is [title] the same as other stories you have read? How is it different?
- Think about the ending of [title]. How is this ending similar to the ending of [title]?

How Leopard Got His Spots, Student Book, Lesson 12

Little Rabbit's Tale, Student Book, Lesson 20

Fable

SUPPORT THINKING

DISCUSSION STARTERS During whole-group and small-group discussion, use questions to spark conversation about genre characteristics.

- Who is this story about?
- What is [character name] like?
- What is happening in this story?
- What problem does [character name] have?
- What does [character name] learn?
- Where is this story happening?
- What can you tell about [character name] by what he/she says? What can you tell about [character name] from the pictures?
- What is the lesson of the story?

COMPARING TEXTS After children have read and listened to several fables, prompt them to compare stories and to recognize common characteristics. Use questions such as these:

- How are the characters in [title] and [title] the same?
- How is [title] the same as other stories you have read?
- How are the lessons the characters learn in [title] and [title] the same?
- How is [title] different from another fable you have read?

City Mouse and Country Mouse, Student Book, Lesson 4

Jack and the Wolf, Student Book, Lesson 6

Genre Characteristics

A fable is a short, made-up story that teaches a lesson.

Through repeated exposure to fables, children should learn to notice common genre characteristics, though at Grade 1 they will not be expected to use the technical labels (except for *characters, setting,* and *lesson*). Use friendly language to help them understand the following concepts:

- **Author's Purpose:** to entertain; to teach a lesson
- **Characters:** the people or animals in a story; characters in fables are often animals or objects that talk and act like people
- **Setting:** where and when the story takes place
- **Plot:** what happens in the story; includes a problem that characters face, what happens as characters try to solve the problem, and an ending
- **Dialogue:** the words that characters say to each other
- **Message/Moral:** the lesson characters learn from what happens in the story

JOURNEYS Literature

STUDENT BOOK	TEACHER'S EDITION READ-ALOUD	LEVELED READERS
City Mouse and Country Mouse	The Lion and the Mouse	Fox and Crow I
Jack and the Wolf	The Tortoise and the Hare	Go Turtle! Go Hare! D
The Wind and the Sun		Turtle and Hare D

Realistic Fiction

Genre Characteristics

Realistic fiction is a made-up story that could happen in real life.

Through repeated exposure to realistic fiction, children should learn to notice common genre characteristics, though at Grade 1 they will not be expected to use the technical labels (except for *characters* and *setting*). Use friendly language to help them understand the following concepts:

- **Author's Purpose:** to entertain
- **Characters:** the people or animals in a story; characters in realistic fiction might remind children of people they know
- **Setting:** where and when the story happens; could be a real place
- **Plot:** what happens in the story; includes a problem that characters face, things that happen as characters try to solve the problem, and an ending
- **Dialogue:** the words that characters say to each other; characters talk like real people

JOURNEYS Literature

STUDENT BOOK
The Dot
A Musical Day
The New Friend
The Storm
Whistle for Willie

TEACHER'S EDITION READ-ALOUD
Around the World in a Day
The Art Contest
Grandpa's Tree
Night of the Wolf
The Piano Lessons
The Rainy Trip

LEVELED READERS
Amy's Airplane **E**
The Beach **J**
The Bumpy Snowman **H**
Dress Up **B**
First Day of Second Grade **H**
Grandpa and Me **C**
Granny **A**
The Lemonade Stand **L**
Len's Tomato Plant **I**
Len's Tomatoes **I**
A Mexican Festival **J**
Molly's New Team **F**
Nana's House **D**
Our Bakery **H**

Our Day at Nana's House **D**
Our Day at the Bakery **H**
Our School **F**
Paco's Snowman **I**
Ready for Second Grade **I**
A Surprise for Ms. Green **J**
Tag-Along Tim **J**
What I Want to Be **J**
When Grandpa Was a Boy **C**
Working in the Park **E**

The Storm, Student Book, Lesson 2   *A Musical Day,* Student Book, Lesson 8

Informational Text

SUPPORT THINKING

DISCUSSION STARTERS During whole-group and small-group discussion, use questions to spark conversation about genre characteristics.

- What is this book about?
- What different kinds of type do you see?
- What kinds of pictures does the author use?
- What can you learn from the pictures?
- What does the author do to make the book interesting?
- How does the author organize the book to help you understand what you are reading?
- How do you know that the information in the book is true?
- How do you think the author feels about the topic? How do you know?

COMPARING TEXTS After children have read and listened to several informational selections, prompt them to compare selections and to recognize common characteristics. Use questions such as these:

- How are the animals in [title] and [title] the same?
- Think about [title] and [title]. How are they the same? How are they different?
- How do the pictures in [title] and [title] help you understand the author's ideas?

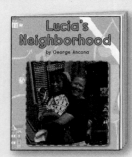 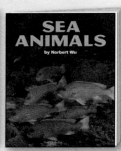

Lucia's Neighborhood, Student Book, Lesson 4

Sea Animals, Student Book, Lesson 11

Genre Characteristics

Informational text gives facts about a topic.

Through repeated exposure to informational text, children should learn to notice common genre characteristics, though at Grade 1 they will not be expected to use the technical labels. Use friendly language to help them understand the following concepts:

- **Author's Purpose:** to inform
- **Graphic Features:** pictures that help the reader understand information or show more about the topic
  - **Diagrams:** pictures with labels
  - **Maps:** pictures that show where something is or how to get from one place to another
  - **Graphs/Charts:** pictures that help readers compare information
- **Text Features:** ways the author makes words stand out
  - **Headings:** type—usually larger, darker, or both—at the beginning of a new section
  - **Captions:** words or sentences that explain a picture
  - **Sizes/Colors:** authors use different sizes and colors to help readers see what is most important
- **Main Idea:** what the book is mostly about
- **Details:** pieces of information that tell more about the main idea or topic
- **Text Structure:** how the book is organized
- **Fact:** a piece of information that is true and can be proved
- **Opinion:** a statement of what the author thinks or believes

JOURNEYS Literature

STUDENT BOOK
Amazing Animals
Animal Groups
Be a Team Player
A Butterfly Grows
City Zoo
Drums
How Animals Communicate
Insect Messages
It Comes from Trees
Let's Go to the Moon!
Life Then and Now
Lucia's Neighborhood
Measuring Weather
Neighborhoods
The Olympic Games
The Rain Forest
School Long Ago

Sea Animals
Seasons
Storms
Water
What Can You Do?
What Is a Pal?
Where Does Food Come From?
Winners Never Quit!

TEACHER'S EDITION READ-ALOUD
A Hopeful Song
One Giant Leap
Prairie Dogs
The Prickly Pride of Texas
Training Around the Town
Visiting Butterflies

LEVELED READERS
Aesop's Fables **K**
All About Bats **J**
All About Fireflies **I**
Always Learning **K**
The Amazing Octopus **L**
Animal Babies **J**
Animal Talk **C**
Animals **E**
Animals at Night **D**
Apples **D**
At the Park **A**
Baby Birds **E**
Baby Kangaroos **I**
Bald Eagles **L**
The Baseball Game **I**
Bear Cubs **J**

JOURNEYS Literature

LEVELED READERS CONT.

Birthdays Around the World J
Busy Animals at Night D
Butterflies F
Butterfly Survival K
Coral Reefs H
Crossing the Ocean K
Curious About School B
Curious About School Helpers G
The Deer Family K
Desert Animals E
Dogs B
Dog Talk J
The Dogwood Tree J
Drawing B
Ducks D
Fall Changes I
Favorite Things B
Fireflies I
Firehouse C
Food for You H
Friends I
Friends Who Share C
A Fun Baseball Game H
Getting Energy from Food K
Going to School E
The Golden Rule K
Good Friends H
Grandpa B
Happy Birthday! C
Helping A
Helping at Home E

Helping Hands J
Honeybees L
How Animals Move J
How We Get Food G
In the Fall H
In the Sea D
In the Sky D
Jim Henson, the Puppet Man E
Jobs to Do J
Kamala's Art H
Kite Flying F
Ladybugs F
Lance Armstrong L
Leopards K
Life in the Coral Reefs G
Living and Working in Space J
Lots of Boats K
Making a Home D
The Man Who Made Puppets E
Many Kinds of Bats J
Marching Bands L
Margret and Hans Rey J
Mia Hamm, Soccer Star J
Michelle Wie F
Moving G
Music C
My Favorite Foods D
Mystery Fruit K
Neighbors I
Our Class E
Our Town C
People in the Town D

A Place in My Town H
The Places in Our Town C
Reading D
Reading Together C
Roadrunner J
Sea Lions J
Seasons I
Seasons Around the World K
The Seasons of the Year I
Sharing C
Shark D
Sink or Float? E
Soccer G
So Many Sounds F
Something Special J
Spots D
The Sun D
Sun, Earth, and Moon L
Tiny Baby Kangaroos I
Trains C
A Train Trip L
Trees G
Two Sisters Play Tennis J
Watercolors A
The Weather E
Whale Songs K
The Williams Sisters J
Wind L
Wind Instruments M
Winter B
A World of Food K
Writers J

Biography

SUPPORT THINKING

DISCUSSION STARTERS During whole-group and small-group discussion, use questions to spark conversation about genre characteristics.

- Who is this book about?
- What is/was [subject name] like?
- What important things happened to [subject name]?
- Where did [subject name] live?
- What did other people think about [subject name]?
- What is the author trying to tell readers about [subject name]?
- Why is it important to know about [subject name]'s life?
- What can you learn from [subject name]'s life?

COMPARING TEXTS After children have read and listened to several biographies, prompt them to compare selections and to recognize common characteristics. Use questions such as these:

- How are [subject name] and [subject name] the same?
- How is [title] the same as other biographies you have read? How is it different?
- Which person would you like to read more about? Explain.
- Of all the biographies you've read, which tells about the most interesting person? Explain.

Dr. Seuss, Student Book, Lesson 9

Mae Jemison, Student Book, Lesson 16

Genre Characteristics

A biography is the true story of a real person's life.

Through repeated exposure to biographies, children should learn to notice common genre characteristics, though at Grade 1 they will not be expected to use the technical labels. Use friendly language to help them understand the following concepts:

- **Author's Purpose:** to inform; to show why this person's life is important
- **Important Events:** told in the order they happened
- **Facts and Opinions:** help readers understand how the author feels and why the person's life is important
- **Narrative Structure:** events told in order as a story; may tell about all or just part of the person's life

JOURNEYS Literature

STUDENT BOOK

Artists Create Art!

Dr. Seuss

Mae Jemison

Tomás Rivera

TEACHER'S EDITION READ-ALOUD

Christina's Work

LEVELED READERS

Jim Henson, The Puppet Man **E**

Lance Armstrong **L**

The Man Who Made Puppets **E**

Margret and Hans Rey **J**

Mia Hamm, Soccer Star **J**

Michelle Wie **F**

Two Sisters Play Tennis **J**

The Williams Sisters **J**

Genre Characteristics

Poetry is a piece of writing in which words are used to show feelings and ideas.

Through repeated exposure to poetry, children should learn to notice common genre characteristics, though at Grade 1 they will not be expected to use the technical labels (except for *rhyme*). Use friendly language to help them understand the following concepts:

- **Author's Purpose:** to entertain; to express
- **Forms:** include traditional rhymes, songs, chants, free verse, and list poems
- **Rhyme:** to have the same ending sound; rhyming words can make a poem fun to read
- **Rhythm:** the beat of how the words are read
- **Sensory Words:** words that describe how things look, feel, taste, smell, and sound
- **Repeated Readings:** can often help readers enjoy and understand a poem more

JOURNEYS Literature

STUDENT BOOK
Busy Bugs
The Four Seasons
Friends Forever

Pet Poems
Silly Poems
Two Poems from Dr. Seuss

TEACHER'S EDITION READ-ALOUD
Painting Word Pictures

SUPPORT THINKING

DISCUSSION STARTERS During whole-group and small-group discussion, use questions to spark conversation about genre characteristics.

- What does this poem tell about?
- Which words in the poem rhyme?
- Which words in the poem help you picture something?
- Which words in the poem describe sounds? Which words describe smells? Which words describe tastes?
- Is the poem silly or serious? How do you know?

COMPARING TEXTS After children have read and listened to several poems, prompt them to compare poems and to recognize common characteristics. Use questions such as these:

- How are [title] and [title] the same?
- How are the poems in [title] the same as other poems you have read?
- How are the poems in *Two Poems from Dr. Seuss* like other things that Dr. Seuss has written?
- Which poem in *The Four Seasons* best helps you picture the season? Explain.

The Four Seasons,
Student Book,
Lesson 13

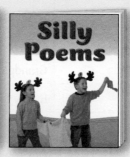

Silly Poems,
Student Book,
Lesson 20

Leveled Readers Database

Guided Reading Level	Title	Grade Pack	DRA Level	Lexile Level	Reading Recovery Level	Genre	Word Count
A	At the Park	1 ●	A	BR	A, B	Informational Text	36
A	Granny	1 ●	A	180	A, B	Realistic Fiction	36
A	Helping	1 ●	1	BR	1	Informational Text	36
A	Sledding	1 ●	A	290	A, B	Fantasy	58
B	Curious About School	1VR	2	20	2	Informational Text	50
B	Curious George Finds Out About School	1 ●	4	60	4	Fantasy	51
B	Dogs	1 ●	2	BR	2	Informational Text	79
B	Drawing	1 ●	2	BR	2	Informational Text	48
B	Dress Up	1 ●	2	BR	2	Realistic Fiction	49
B	Favorite Things	1VR	2	BR	2	Informational Text	47
B	Grandpa	1VR	2	50	2	Informational Text	50
B	Pigs, The	1 ●	2	BR	2	Fable	83
B	Trip to the Rock	1 ●	2	130	2	Fantasy	90
B	Winter	1 ●	2	20	2	Informational Text	79
C	Animal Talk	1VR	3	240	3	Informational Text	55
C	Curious George Visits School	1 ◆	4	140	4	Fantasy	88
C	Curious George's Day at School	1 ▲	4	140	4	Fantasy	87
C	Firehouse	1VR	3	BR	3	Informational Text	58
C	Friends Who Share	1 ◆	4	180	4	Informational Text	118
C	Grandpa and Me	1 ▲	3	420	3	Realistic Fiction	86
C	Happy Birthday!	1VR	4	BR	4	Informational Text	78
C	Music	1VR	3	BR	3	Informational Text	58
C	Our Town	1 ▲	3	240	3	Informational Text	103
C	Places in Our Town, The	1 ◆	6	200	6	Informational Text	108
C	Reading Together	1VR	4	BR	4	Informational Text	62
C	Sharing	1 ▲	4	100	4	Informational Text	107
C	Trains	1VR	3	150	3	Informational Text	65
C	When Grandpa Was a Boy	1 ◆	4	450	4	Realistic Fiction	93
D	Animals at Night	1 ▲	6	220	6	Informational Text	161
D	Apples	1 ●	6	240	5	Informational Text	100

ONLINE LEVELED READERS DATABASE

- Go to www.thinkcentral.com for the complete *Journeys* Online Leveled Readers Database.
- Search by grade, genre, title, or level.

Author's Purpose	Cause and Effect	Compare and Contrast	Conclusions	Fact and Opinion	Main Idea and Details	Sequence of Events	Story Structure	Text and Graphic Features	Theme	Understanding Characters
				●	●			●		
		●				●				●
●	●				●					
	●					●	●			●
●					●					
	●					●			●	●
		●		●	●			●		
	●		●		●	●		●		
	●		●			●				●
●	●		●	●	●					
●		●			●					
						●				●
			●			●	●			
●	●		●		●	●				
●			●		●					
	●					●			●	●
	●					●			●	●
●					●					
●					●					
●		●	●			●			●	●
●					●					
●			●		●			●		
●	●				●			●		
●					●			●		
●					●					
●					●					
●					●					
		●							●	●
					●			●		
●					●					

Leveled Readers Database

Guided Reading Level	Title	Grade Pack	DRA Level	Lexile Level	Reading Recovery Level	Genre	Word Count
D	Ben the Cat	1 ▲	6	90	6	Fantasy	124
D	Busy Animals at Night	1 ◆	6	270	5	Informational Text	183
D	Cat Named Ben, A	1 ◆	6	70	5	Fantasy	131
D	Ducks	1VR	6	30	5	Informational Text	65
D	Go Turtle! Go Hare!	1 ◆	6	80	5	Fable	100
D	In the Sea	1 ●	6	360	5	Informational Text	87
D	In the Sky	1VR	6	120	6	Informational Text	101
D	Izzy's Move	1 ●	6	290	6	Fantasy	129
D	Making a Home	1 ●	6	220	6	Informational Text	102
D	My Favorite Foods	1VR	6	130	6	Informational Text	95
D	Nana's House	1 ▲	6	320	6	Realistic Fiction	133
D	Our Day at Nana's House	1 ◆	6	330	5	Realistic Fiction	137
D	People in the Town	1VR	6	140	5	Informational Text	107
D	Putting Frosting on the Cake	1 ●	6	360	6	Fantasy	120
D	Reading	1VR	6	80	6	Informational Text	76
D	Shark	1VR	6	20	6	Informational Text	85
D	Spots	1VR	6	90	6	Informational Text	83
D	Sun, The	1 ●	6	BR	5	Informational Text	119
D	Turtle and Hare	1 ▲	6	40	6	Fable	94
E	Amy's Airplane	1 ●	8	270	8	Realistic Fiction	147
E	Animal Homes	1 ●	8	170	8	Informational Text	170
E	Animals	1VR	8	190	7	Informational Text	115
E	Baby Birds	1VR	8	270	8	Informational Text	180
E	Bear Swims	1 ●	8	240	7	Fantasy	151
E	Desert Animals	1VR	8	330	8	Informational Text	171
E	Going to School	1VR	8	270	7	Informational Text	114
E	Giraffe's Neck	1 ●	8	310	8	Folktale	109
E	Happy Birthday, Toad	1 ◆	8	270	7	Fantasy	144
E	Helping at Home	1VR	8	380	7	Informational Text	158
E	Jim Henson, the Puppet Man	1 ▲	8	200	7	Informational Text	93

ONLINE LEVELED READERS DATABASE

- Go to www.thinkcentral.com for the complete *Journeys* Online Leveled Readers Database.
- Search by grade, genre, title, or level.

Author's Purpose	Cause and Effect	Compare and Contrast	Conclusions	Fact and Opinion	Main Idea and Details	Sequence of Events	Story Structure	Text and Graphic Features	Theme	Understanding Characters
			●			●	●			●
					●			●		
			●			●	●			●
●			●		●					
●	●	●	●			●	●		●	●
●					●	●				
●		●			●					
	●	●	●			●	●		●	
●	●			●				●		
●	●	●	●		●					
	●		●			●				●
	●		●			●				●
●		●	●		●					
	●		●			●	●			●
●		●		●	●					
					●			●		
●					●					
					●			●		
●	●	●	●			●	●		●	●
	●		●			●	●			●
●			●		●					
●		●	●		●					
●					●					
		●					●			●
●		●	●		●					
●			●		●					
●	●					●	●			
						●	●			
●			●		●					
●				●	●				●	

Leveled Readers Database

Guided Reading Level	Title	Grade Pack	DRA Level	Lexile Level	Reading Recovery Level	Genre	Word Count
E	Man Who Made Puppets, The	1 ◆	8	350	8	Informational Text	106
E	Our Class	1 ●	8	190	7	Informational Text	200
E	Seed for Sid, A	1 ●	8	280	8	Fantasy	131
E	Sink or Float?	1VR	8	140	8	Informational Text	161
E	Toad's Birthday	1 ▲	8	230	8	Fantasy	135
E	Weather, The	1VR	8	290	8	Informational Text	81
E	Working in the Park	1 ●	8	380	8	Realistic Fiction	118
F	Butterflies	1VR	10	470	9	Informational Text	180
F	Chunk of Cheese, A	1 ●	10	370	10	Fantasy	215
F	Kite Flying	1VR	10	440	9	Informational Text	192
F	Ladybugs	1 ●	10	510	9	Informational Text	163
F	Michelle Wie	1 ●	10	120	10	Narrative Nonfiction	153
F	Missing Glove, The	1 ●	10	120	9	Mystery	212
F	Molly's New Team	1 ●	10	180	10	Realistic Fiction	161
F	Our School	1 ●	10	350	9	Realistic Fiction	182
F	So Many Sounds	1VR	10	400	10	Informational Text	166
G	Curious About School Helpers	1CY	12	270	12	Informational Text	203
G	How We Get Food	1 ◆	12	320	12	Informational Text	291
G	Life in the Coral Reefs	1 ◆	12	430	12	Informational Text	198
G	Moving	1VR	12	170	12	Informational Text	170
G	Polly's Pet Polar Bear	1 ◆	12	300	12	Fantasy	279
G	Skunk Cooks Soup	1 ◆	12	350	12	Fantasy	299
G	Soccer	1VR	12	510	12	Informational Text	201
G	Trees	1VR	12	350	12	Informational Text	156
H	Bear's Long, Brown Tail	1 ◆	14	250	14	Folktale	332
H	Bear's Tail	1 ▲	14	480	14	Folktale	292
H	Bumpy Snowman, The	1 ◆	14	370	14	Realistic Fiction	334
H	Coral Reefs	1 ▲	14	570	13	Informational Text	203
H	First Day of Second Grade	1 ◆	14	360	14	Realistic Fiction	263
H	Flying	1 ▲	14	390	13	Fantasy	226

ONLINE LEVELED READERS DATABASE

- Go to www.thinkcentral.com for the complete *Journeys* Online Leveled Readers Database.
- Search by grade, genre, title, or level.

Author's Purpose	Cause and Effect	Compare and Contrast	Conclusions	Fact and Opinion	Main Idea and Details	Sequence of Events	Story Structure	Text and Graphic Features	Theme	Understanding Characters
●				●	●			●		
					●			●		
			●			●	●			
●					●					
						●	●			
●					●					
			●			●				
●			●		●					
	●		●			●	●		●	
●					●					
●					●	●				
●					●					●
	●		●			●	●			●
						●	●		●	●
		●	●							●
●			●		●					
●	●				●					
●	●				●					
●				●	●			●		
●					●					
	●						●			●
●	●					●	●		●	
●					●					
●		●			●					
●	●	●	●			●	●		●	●
●	●	●	●			●	●		●	●
●	●	●	●			●	●		●	●
●				●	●			●		
			●			●	●			●
		●				●	●		●	●

Leveled Readers Database

Guided Reading Level	Title	Grade Pack	DRA Level	Lexile Level	Reading Recovery Level	Genre	Word Count
H	Flying in an Airplane	1 ◆	14	200	14	Fantasy	272
H	Food for You	1 ▲	14	440	14	Informational Text	232
H	Forest Stew	1 ▲	14	380	14	Fantasy	239
H	Fun Baseball Game, A	1 ◆	14	480	13	Informational Text	376
H	Good Friends	1CY	14	280	14	Informational Text	169
H	In the Fall	1 ◆	14	300	14	Informational Text	286
H	Kamala's Art	1VR	14	430	13	Informational Text	184
H	Our Bakery	1 ▲	14	380	14	Realistic Fiction	230
H	Our Day at the Bakery	1 ◆	14	210	14	Realistic Fiction	274
H	Place in My Town, A	1CY	14	180	14	Informational Text	184
H	Polar Bear Pete	1 ▲	14	480	14	Fantasy	273
H	Where Is Cow's Lunch?	1 ◆	14	200	14	Mystery	321
I	All About Fireflies	1 ◆	16	400	16	Informational Text	319
I	Baby Kangaroos	1 ▲	16	540	15	Informational Text	256
I	Baseball Game, The	1 ▲	16	540	16	Informational Text	358
I	Chipmunk's New Home	1 ■	16	400	16	Fantasy	300
I	Cow's Lunch	1 ▲	16	340	16	Mystery	363
I	Curious George at the Library	1 ■	16	280	16	Fantasy	281
I	Fall Changes	1 ▲	16	460	16	Informational Text	320
I	Fireflies	1 ▲	16	530	15	Informational Text	289
I	Fox and Crow	1 ■	16	380	15	Fable	333
I	Friends	1 ■	16	400	15	Informational Text	302
I	Len's Tomato Plant	1 ◆	16	380	15	Realistic Fiction	294
I	Len's Tomatoes	1 ▲	16	430	15	Realistic Fiction	289
I	Map and the Treasure, The	1 ◆	16	300	15	Fantasy	292
I	Marching Bands	1CY	16	470	16	Informational Text	166
I	Neighbors	1 ■	16	330	15	Informational Text	244
I	Paco's Snowman	1 ▲	16	380	16	Realistic Fiction	330
I	Ready for Second Grade	1 ▲	16	360	15	Realistic Fiction	295
I	Seasons	1 ▲	16	400	15	Informational Text	253

ONLINE LEVELED READERS DATABASE

- Go to www.thinkcentral.com for the complete *Journeys* Online Leveled Readers Database.
- Search by grade, genre, title, or level.

Author's Purpose	Cause and Effect	Compare and Contrast	Conclusions	Fact and Opinion	Main Idea and Details	Sequence of Events	Story Structure	Text and Graphic Features	Theme	Understanding Characters
		●				●	●		●	●
●	●				●					
●	●					●	●		●	
				●	●	●		●		
●	●			●	●					
	●	●			●	●				
●					●					
	●		●			●				
●	●		●			●				
●			●	●	●			●		
	●						●			●
	●			●		●	●			●
●					●	●		●		
●			●		●	●				
				●	●	●		●		
	●					●	●			
	●		●			●	●			●
	●					●	●			●
	●	●			●	●				
●					●	●		●		
●	●					●	●		●	●
●	●	●			●					
●	●					●				
●	●					●				
●	●		●			●	●		●	
●		●		●	●					
								●		
●	●	●	●			●	●		●	●
			●			●	●			●
●			●		●			●		

Leveled Readers Database

Guided Reading Level	Title	Grade Pack	DRA Level	Lexile Level	Reading Recovery Level	Genre	Word Count
I	Seasons of the Year, The	1 ◆	16	430	16	Informational Text	332
I	Tiny Baby Kangaroos	1 ◆	16	620	15	Informational Text	296
I	Train Trip, A	1CY	16	420	16	Informational Text	172
I	Treasure Map, The	1 ▲	16	320	15	Fantasy	306
J	All About Bats	1 ▲	18	520	18	Informational Text	296
J	Animal Babies	1CY	18	580	18	Informational Text	369
J	Beach, The	1 ■	18	320	18	Realistic Fiction	292
J	Bear Cubs	1CY	18	480	18	Informational Text	408
J	Birthdays Around the World	1CY	18	510	18	Informational Text	178
J	Boat Race, The	1 ◆	18	380	18	Fantasy	366
J	Bobcat Tells a Tale	1 ■	18	310	18	Fantasy	255
J	Dog Talk	1 ■	18	310	18	Informational Text	324
J	Dogwood Tree, The	1CY	18	680	18	Informational Text	363
J	Helping Hands	1CY	18	530	18	Informational Text	387
J	How Animals Move	1 ■	18	650	18	Informational Text	401
J	Job for Jojo, A	1 ■	18	210	18	Fantasy	326
J	Jobs to Do	1CY	18	430	18	Informational Text	368
J	Lena's Garden	1 ■	18	590	18	Fantasy	302
J	Living and Working in Space	1 ■	18	650	18	Informational Text	383
J	Many Kinds of Bats	1 ◆	18	530	18	Informational Text	292
J	Margret and Hans Rey	1 ■	18	520	18	Informational Text	237
J	Mexican Festival, A	1 ■	18	340	18	Realistic Fiction	267
J	Mia Hamm, Soccer Star	1CY	18	650	18	Informational Text	390
J	Mountain, The	1 ■	18	320	18	Fantasy	348
J	Roadrunner	1CY	18	640	18	Informational Text	353
J	Sailboat Race, The	1 ▲	18	330	18	Fantasy	330
J	Sea Lions	1CY	18	620	18	Informational Text	316
J	Something Special	1CY	18	170	18	Informational Text	207
J	Surprise for Ms. Green, A	1 ■	18	300	18	Realistic Fiction	393
J	Tag-Along Tim	1 ■	18	410	18	Realistic Fiction	358

ONLINE LEVELED READERS DATABASE

- Go to www.thinkcentral.com for the complete *Journeys* Online Leveled Readers Database.
- Search by grade, genre, title, or level.

Author's Purpose	Cause and Effect	Compare and Contrast	Conclusions	Fact and Opinion	Main Idea and Details	Sequence of Events	Story Structure	Text and Graphic Features	Theme	Understanding Characters
•			•		•			•		
•			•		•	•				
•					•			•		
•	•		•			•	•		•	
•		•			•			•		
•		•			•					
•			•			•				
•	•				•	•				
•		•		•	•			•		
•	•		•			•	•		•	•
	•		•			•	•			
•					•					
•		•		•	•	•		•		
•	•		•		•	•				
•			•		•			•		
			•			•	•			•
•	•	•		•	•					
	•		•				•	•		•
•	•				•			•		
•		•			•			•		
•					•			•		
						•				•
•	•				•					
		•				•	•			
•	•		•	•		•				
•	•		•			•	•		•	•
•	•				•			•		
•				•	•					
		•	•				•		•	•
•			•			•	•		•	•

Leveled Readers Database

Guided Reading Level	Title	Grade Pack	DRA Level	Lexile Level	Reading Recovery Level	Genre	Word Count
J	Two Sisters Play Tennis	1 ◆	18	480	18	Narrative Nonfiction	327
J	What I Want to Be	1 ■	18	320	18	Realistic Fiction	377
J	Williams Sisters, The	1 ▲	18	450	18	Narrative Nonfiction	318
J	Writers	1CY	18	450	18	Informational Text	264
K	Aesop's Fables	1CY	20	530	18	Informational Text	209
K	Always Learning	1 ■	20	480	18	Informational Text	392
K	Barnyard Bandit, The	1 ■	20	440	18	Mystery	371
K	Butterfly Survival	1CY	20	600	18	Informational Text	329
K	Cam the Camel	1 ■	20	440	18	Fantasy	334
K	Crossing the Ocean	1CY	20	660	18	Informational Text	374
K	Deer Family, The	1CY	20	690	18	Informational Text	412
K	Getting Energy from Food	1CY	20	520	18	Informational Text	283
K	Golden Rule, The	1CY	20	510	18	Informational Text	360
K	Leopards	1CY	20	590	18	Informational Text	343
K	Lots of Boats	1CY	20	510	18	Informational Text	468
K	Mystery Fruit	1CY	20	400	18	Informational Text	364
K	Sand Castle, The	1 ■	20	370	18	Fantasy	388
K	Seasons Around the World	1 ■	20	600	18	Informational Text	353
K	Watercolors	1CY	20	560	18	Informational Text	369
K	Whale Songs	1CY	20	520	18	Informational Text	173
K	World of Food, A	1 ■	20	580	18	Informational Text	340
L	Amazing Octopus, The	1 ■	24	520	20	Informational Text	346
L	Bald Eagles	1 ■	24	640	20	Informational Text	420
L	Honeybees	1 ■	24	700	20	Informational Text	379
L	Lance Armstrong	1 ■	24	540	20	Narrative Nonfiction	444
L	Lemonade Stand, The	1 ■	24	560	20	Realistic Fiction	386
L	Peacock's Tail	1 ■	24	530	20	Folktale	344
L	Sun, Earth, and Moon	1CY	24	520	20	Informational Text	391
L	Wind	1CY	24	640	20	Informational Text	430
M	Wind Instruments	1CY	28	630	20	Informational Text	391

ONLINE LEVELED READERS DATABASE

- Go to www.thinkcentral.com for the complete *Journeys* Online Leveled Readers Database.
- Search by grade, genre, title, or level.

Author's Purpose	Cause and Effect	Compare and Contrast	Conclusions	Fact and Opinion	Main Idea and Details	Sequence of Events	Story Structure	Text and Graphic Features	Theme	Understanding Characters
●					●					●
	●	●	●							
●					●					●
●			●	●	●					
●				●	●					
●				●	●	●		●		
	●		●				●		●	
●		●	●	●	●	●		●		
			●			●	●		●	●
●		●		●	●					
●		●			●					
●	●			●	●	●		●		
●	●		●		●					
●	●	●		●	●					
●		●			●	●				
●	●		●	●	●	●		●		
	●					●	●		●	●
●	●	●			●					
●	●			●	●	●		●		
●			●	●						
●					●			●		
●	●			●	●					
●		●		●	●					
●	●			●	●	●		●		
●	●			●	●	●				●
	●					●	●			
●	●	●	●			●	●		●	●
●				●	●			●		
●	●		●	●	●					
	●	●		●	●			●		

Literature Discussion

For small-group literature discussion, use the suggested trade book titles on the pages that follow, or select age-appropriate texts from your library or classroom collection.

Engage children in discussions to build understanding of the text, deepen comprehension, and foster children's confidence in talking about what they read. Encourage children to share their ideas about the text and also to build upon one another's ideas.

 Classic

 Science

 Social Studies

 Music

 Math

 Art

Suggested Trade Book Titles

BIOGRAPHY

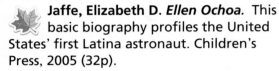 **Carson, Cheryl. *Charles M. Schultz.*** Cartoonist Charles M. Schultz is profiled here. Capstone Press, 2005 (24p).

Jaffe, Elizabeth D. *Ellen Ochoa.* This basic biography profiles the United States' first Latina astronaut. Children's Press, 2005 (32p).

Knox, Barbara. *George Washington.* This easy-to-read introduction to the life of George Washington includes a timeline. Capstone, 2004 (24p).

Krensky, Stephen. *A Man for All Seasons: The Life of George Washington Carver.* This biography profiles the man whose discoveries put the peanut on the map. Amistad, 2008 (32p).

Marzolla, Jean, and Jerry Pinkney. *Happy Birthday, Martin Luther King.* This brief narrative of Dr. King's life is presented in an easy-to-read format. Scholastic, 1993 (32p).

FABLE

Herman, Gail. *The Lion and the Mouse.* This fable is an easy-to-read retelling of Aesop's classic tale. Random House, 1998 (32p).

Poole, Amy Lowry. *The Ant and the Grasshopper.* Grasshopper plays the summer days away while Ant works hard to prepare for winter. Holiday House, 2000 (32p).

FAIRY TALE

Andersen, Hans Christian, and Jerry Pinkney. *The Ugly Duckling.* Hans Christian Andersen's classic tale is illustrated with Caldecott Honor–winning illustrations. Harper, 1999 (40p).

Gorbachev, Valeri. *Goldilocks and the Three Bears.* Three bears return home to discover an unexpected visitor in their home in this appealing retelling of the classic tale. North-South/Night Sky, 2001 (40p).

FANTASY

Andersen, Peggy Perry. *Chuck's Band.* Chuck and his barnyard friends form a band in this toe-tapping story. Houghton Mifflin, 2008 (32p).

Arnold, Tedd. *Hi! Fly Guy.* A boy goes out searching for a smart animal to take to The Amazing Pet Show and bumps into a fly that is intelligent enough to say the child's name, Buzz. **Available in Spanish as *¡Hola, supermosca!/Hi, Fly Guy.*** Scholastic, 2005 (32p).

Bang-Campbell, Monika. *Little Rat Makes Music.* With the help of Kitty and lots of practice, Little Rat learns to play the violin. Harcourt, 2007 (48p).

Banks, Kate. *Fox.* A baby fox observes the changing seasons while his parents teach him to care for himself. Farrar, Straus and Giroux, 2007 (40p).

Brett, Jan. *Honey. . . Honey. . . Lion!* When greedy Badger will not share honey with his friend, his friend has a surprise for him. Putnam, 2005 (32p).

Campoy, F. Isabel. *Get Up, Rick!* Brief text and supportive illustrations describe what happens on a farm when the rooster oversleeps. Green Light Readers, 2007 (24p).

Carle, Eric. *The Very Hungry Caterpillar.* A caterpillar eats its way through the week and turns into a beautiful butterfly. Philomel, 1969 (32p).

Cazet, Denys. *Minnie and Moo and the Case of the Missing Jelly Donut.* The brave bovine buddies are on the case when Minnie discovers that her jelly donut has gone missing. HarperTrophy, 2006 (48p).

Chaconas, Dori. *Cork and Fuzz: Good Sports.* Two friends learn a lesson about sportsmanship when they compete against one another. Viking, 2007 (32p).

Cronin, Doreen. *Dooby Dooby Moo.* Determined Duck and the rest of Farmer Brown's animals set their sights on first prize at the county fair's talent show, unbeknownst to Farmer Brown. **Available in Spanish as *Dubi Dubi Muu/Dooby Dooby Moo.*** Atheneum, 2006 (40p).

Cyrus, Kurt. *Tadpole Rex.* In a swamp frequented by dinosaurs, a tiny tadpole looks forward to growing as big as his mighty neighbors. Harcourt, 2008 (40p).

DiCamillo, Kate. *Mercy Watson to the Rescue.* When Mr. and Mrs. Watson find themselves in trouble, their pig, Mercy, saves the day. Candlewick, 2005 (80p).

Henkes, Kevin. *A Good Day.* Four animals triumph when they find they can turn a potentially bad day into a good day. Greenwillow, 2007 (32p).

Henkes, Kevin. *Lilly's Big Day.* High-spirited Lilly is disappointed when she is not asked to be the flower girl in her teacher's wedding, but she still finds a way to shine. Greenwillow, 2006 (40p).

Hill, Susan. *Ruby Paints a Picture.* Ruby captures the best part of each of her animal friends in her artwork. HarperCollins, 2005 (32p).

Howe, James. *Houndsley and Catina.* In this early chapter book, a cat and a dog explore ways of sharing themselves and realize that doing what they love is most important. Candlewick, 2006 (40p).

Inkpen, Mick. *Kipper's A to Z: An Alphabet Adventure.* In this innovative alphabet book, Kipper and his little friend Arnold search for things that begin with each letter of the alphabet. Red Wagon, 2001 (56p).

Johnson, Crockett. *Harold and the Purple Crayon.* Harold and his purple crayon go on a whimsical journey in this classic tribute to the imagination. **Available in Spanish as *Harold y el lápiz color morado.*** HarperCollins, 1955 (64p).

Kreloff, Elliot. *Tic and Tac Clean Up.* Once their house is clean, Tic and Tac try to come up with activities that won't make a mess. Sterling, 2007 (32p).

Kvasnosky, Laura McGee. *Zelda and Ivy and the Boy Next Door.* A new neighbor gives fox sisters Zelda and Ivy an opportunity to embark on new capers in this early chapter book. Candlewick, 2008 (48p).

Lies, Brian. *Bats at the Beach.* A typical day at the beach is turned on its head when a family of bats sets out for the sand and sea—at night! Houghton Mifflin, 2006 (32p).

Lionni, Leo. *Swimmy.* Swimmy teaches a school of little fish to swim together to avoid danger in this Caldecott Honor book. **Available in Spanish as *Nadarín.*** Knopf, 1963 (32p).

Lobel, Anita. *Nini Here and There.* Nini the cat fears her family is going away without her but soon learns they would never dream of leaving her behind. Greenwillow, 2007 (32p).

Lobel, Arnold. *Frog and Toad All Year.* The beloved friends enjoy adventures and happy times together during every season of the year. **Available in Spanish as *Sapo y sepo, un año entero.*** HarperCollins, 1976 (64p).

Lucas, Sally. *Dancing Dinos Go to School.* It's an exciting day at school when two irrepressible dinosaurs dance into the classroom in this rhyming story. Random House, 2006 (32p).

McCloskey, Robert. *Make Way for Ducklings.* Follow the Mallard family on their journey through Boston in this children's classic. Viking, 1941 (68p).

McMillan, Bruce. *How the Ladies Stopped the Wind.* A group of resourceful ladies from Iceland use their problem-solving skills to stop the wind. Houghton Mifflin, 2007 (32p).

McMullan, Kate. *I'm Dirty.* With sound words and great enthusiasm, a hard-working backhoe describes how he helps keep his neighborhood clean. Joanna Cotler, 2006 (40p).

Noble, Trinka Hakes. *The Day Jimmy's Boa Ate the Wash.* A school field trip to a farm is full of hilarious surprises when Jimmy brings his pet boa along. Dial, 1980 (32p).

Numeroff, Laura. *If You Give a Pig a Party.* A pig's request to throw a party sets off a chain of funny and unexpected consequences. **Available in Spanish as *Si le haces una fiesta a una cerdita.*** HarperCollins, 2005 (32p).

Pinkwater, Daniel. *Bear's Picture.* Bear stands up for himself when two fine gentlemen criticize his picture. Houghton Mifflin, 2008 (32p).

Rankin, Laura. *Fluffy and Baron.* A duckling and a German shepherd form an unlikely friendship in this gentle story about growing up. Dial, 2006 (32p).

Seuss, Dr. *The Cat in the Hat.* Chaos ensues when the Cat in the Hat pays a visit to Sally and her brother. **Available in Spanish as *El gato en el sombrero/The Cat in the Hat.*** Random House, 1957 (60p).

Seuss, Dr. *Oh, the Thinks You Can Think!* This Seuss classic describes all the imaginative things you can think, if only you try. Random House, 1975 (48p).

Shannon, George. *Rabbit's Gift.* Rabbit shares his winter store of food with friends and starts a wave of generosity that spreads among all the forest animals. Harcourt, 2007 (32p).

Shaw, Nancy. *Sheep Blast Off!* When a spacecraft lands in a nearby field, the lovable, blundering sheep go on board and embark on the ride of their lives. Houghton Mifflin, 2008 (32p).

Sherry, Kevin. *I'm the Biggest Thing in the Ocean.* In this lighthearted tale, a giant squid repeatedly announces that it's the biggest thing in the ocean . . . until it meets an even bigger whale. Dial, 2007 (32p).

Thomas, Jan. *What Will FAT CAT Sit On?* Familiar animals, repetitive text, and humor make this book ideal for new readers. Harcourt, 2007 (40p).

Literature Discussion

Walsh, Ellen Stoll. *Dot & Jabber and the Big Bug Mystery.* Dot and Jabber investigate a field where all the bugs seem to have disappeared and discover that they have all been camouflaged. Harcourt, 2003 (40p).

Willems, Mo. *There Is a Bird on Your Head!* Gerald is surprised to discover that a bird has made itself at home on his head. Hyperion, 2007 (64p).

FOLKTALE

Barton, Byron. *The Little Red Hen.* The little red hen finds that none of her lazy friends want to help her with chores, but all are happy to help her share the rewards. HarperFestival, 1997 (32p).

Bruchac, Joseph. *The Great Ball Game: A Muskogee Story.* When birds and animals challenge each other to a ball game to prove who is better, Bat shows that he has special qualities from both groups. Dial, 1994 (32p).

Demi. *The Empty Pot.* Honesty makes a Chinese boy the winner of the Emperor's flower-growing contest when he admits that he couldn't get his seed to grow. Holt, 1996 (32p).

Tolstoy, Alexei. *The Enormous Turnip.* One by one, family members help pull the enormous turnip out of the ground. Harcourt, 2003 (24p).

Tuchman, Gail. *How the Sky Got Its Stars: A Hopi Legend.* A Hopi legend tells how all animals, except for Coyote, create things on Earth until Coyote plays with the stars and makes something, too. Harcourt, 1997 (16p).

INFORMATIONAL TEXT

Ada, Alma Flor. *I Love Saturdays y domingos.* Weekends are special for a girl who spends time with both her English-speaking grandparents and her Spanish-speaking ones. **Available in Spanish as** *Me encantan los Saturdays y Domingos.* Atheneum, 2002 (32p).

Ajmera, Maya and John D. Ivanko. *Be My Neighbor.* This photo essay shows kids all over the world in the communities they call home. Charlesbridge, 2005 (32p).

Arnold, Katya. *Elephants Can Paint Too!* This profile describes an unusual conservation project, in which an art teacher teaches a group of elephants in Thailand to paint. Atheneum/Anne Schwartz, 2005 (40p).

Arnosky, Jim. *Babies in the Bayou.* This is a clearly illustrated introduction to the littlest inhabitants of the Southern marshland habitat. Penguin, 2007 (32p).

Bauer, Marion Dane. *Clouds.* Clear text presents basic facts about cirrus, stratus, and cumulus clouds for young readers. Tandem, 2004 (32p).

Clements, Andrew. *Tara and Tiree, Fearless Friends: A True Story.* This true story tells how two loyal dogs rescued their owner from a frozen lake. Aladdin, 2003 (32p).

DeGezelle, Terri. *Snowplows.* Easy-to-read text and color photographs introduce children to what snowplows can do. **Avaliable in Spanish as** *Barredoras de nieve/Snowplows.* Capstone, 2006 (24p).

Endres, Hollie J. *Fair Share.* Readers are introduced to the concept of division in this book about sharing. Capstone Press, 2005 (16p).

Gray, Susan Heinrichs. *Dinosaur Dig!* Readers find out what it is like to go on a dinosaur dig. Children's Press, 2007 (24p).

Helbrough, Emma. *How Flowers Grow.* Photographs and diagrams are featured in this description of how flowers grow. Usborne, 2007 (32p).

Jenkins, Martin. *The Emperor's Egg.* This colorful book chronicles how the male emperor penguin keeps his egg warm for two months in subzero temperatures while he waits for his mate's return. Candlewick, 2008 (32p).

Jones, Melanie Davis. *BIG Machines.* Simple text introduces different machines at work in a community. Children's Press, 2003 (24p).

Kalman, Bobbie. *Animals Grow and Change.* Color photographs and informative text introduce the growth cycles of animals. Crabtree, 2007 (24p).

Kalman, Bobbie. *A Forest Habitat.* Photos of baby animals in their natural surroundings help to inform children about forest habitats. **Available in Spanish as** *Un habitat de bosque.* Crabtree, 2006 (32p).

Kenah, Katharine. *Big Beasts.* Photographs and "extreme facts" will keep readers turning the pages in this book about the biggest animals on earth. School Specialty, 2007 (32p).

Lock, David. *Animals at Home.* Readers are introduced to different kinds of homes that animals make for themselves. DK Children, 2007 (32p).

Lock, Deborah. *Let's Make Music.* Informative text supported by photographs describes ways people make music. DK Children, 2005 (32p).

Milbourne, Anna, and Benji Davies. *On the Moon.* Readers take a trip with an astronaut in this friendly intro–duction to the moon. Usborne, 2004 (24p).

Murphy, Patricia J. *Let's Play Soccer.* Erik has fun at his first day of soccer practice. DK Children, 2008 (32p).

Nelson, Robin. *Communication Then and Now.* Readers compare current methods of communication with those of years ago. Lerner, 2003 (24p).

Peterson, Cris. *Fantastic Farm Machines.* A farming family describes machines that help them grow and harvest crops. Boyds Mills, 2006 (32p).

Rau, Dana Meachen. *Buzz, Bee, Buzz!* Bright, colorful photographs and a word list are features of this simple introduction to the bee. **Available in Spanish as** *Zumba, abeja, zumba.* Marshall Cavendish, 2007 (24p).

Rau, Dana Meachen. *Firefighter.* Simple text and rebuses provide an easy-to-read introduction to the job of a firefighter. **Available in Spanish as** *Un bombero.* Marshall Cavendish, 2007 (24p).

Ring, Susan. *From Here to There.* Photographs and informative text explore the different ways people travel. **Available in Spanish as** *De aquí a allá.* Yellow Umbrella, 2004 (16p).

Rotner, Shelley. *Senses at the Seashore.* This photo essay with minimal text evokes the sights, sounds, and smells of the seashore. Millbrook, 2005 (32p).

Ryder, Joanne. *A Pair of Polar Bears.* Twin polar bear cubs play, learn, and grow at the San Diego Zoo. Simon & Schuster, 2006 (32p).

Stone, Lynn M. *How Do Animals Use Their Voices and Sound?* Simple text and color photographs depict what various animals have to say. **Available in Spanish as** *¿Cómo usan los animales su vos y sus sonidos?* Rourke, 2007 (24p).

Time for Kids with Brenda Iasevoli. *Time for Kids: Plants!* Photos and informative text give facts about plants. HarperCollins, 2006 (32p).

Time for Kids with Leslie Dickstein. *Time for Kids: Storms!* Vivid photos complement the informative text about severe weather. HarperCollins, 2006 (32p).

Udry, Janet May. *A Tree Is Nice.* Poetic text reveals the reasons trees are so nice. **Available in Spanish as** *Un árbol es hermoso.* Harper, 1956 (32p).

VanVoorst, Jennifer. *Can You Guess?* Colorful photographs and informative text introduce the concept of estimation. Yellow Umbrella, 2004 (16p).

Wallace, Karen. *Rockets and Spaceships.* Photographs and informative text provide an exciting look at the technology that makes space exploration possible. Dorling Kindersley, 2001 (32p).

POETRY

Brown, Richard. *Street Music.* Rhythmic text and lively illustrations introduce readers to the music of the city. Sterling, 2006 (24p).

Crews, Nina. *The Neighborhood Mother Goose.* Traditional Mother Goose rhymes are paired with colorful photographs of children in this award-winning collection. Amistad, 2003 (64p).

Ehlert, Lois. *Oodles of Animals.* Playful rhymes and bold illustrations capture the spirit of 64 different animals. Harcourt, 2008 (56p).

Falwell, Cathryn. *Scoot!* Collage artwork and spirited action words introduce the inhabitants of a lively pond habitat. Greenwillow, 2008 (32p).

Lansky, Bruce. *I Hope I Don't Strike Out.* A collection of silly poems that focuses on the funny side of sports. Meadowbrook, 2008 (32p).

Lillegard, Dee. *Go! Poetry in Motion.* A lively collection of poetry featuring rhyme and sound words that celebrates the ways we get from here to there. Knopf, 2006 (32p).

Lumley, Jemima. *The Journey Home from Grandpa's.* A family enjoys the sights as they travel from the country to the city in this rhythmic story. Barefoot Books, 2006 (24p).

Mora, Pat. *Yum! Mmmm! Qué Rico!: America's Sproutings.* This poetry collection is a delicious introduction to fourteen types of food that grow. **Available in Spanish as** *Yum! ¡MmMm! ¡Qué rico! Brotes de las Américas.* Lee & Low, 2007 (32p).

Prelutsky, Jack. *My Dog May Be a Genius.* This collection of silly poems is sure to make readers giggle. Greenwillow, 2008 (160p).

Roemer, Heidi. *Come to My Party and Other Shape Poems.* Playful poems featuring sound words and repetition describe seasonal activities. Henry Holt and Co., 2004 (32p).

REALISTIC FICTION

Adler, David A. *Young Cam Jansen and the Lions' Lunch Mystery.* Young Cam Jansen uses her sleuthing skills to find a lost lunch bag on a school trip to the zoo. Viking, 2007 (32p).

dePaola, Tomie. *The Art Lesson.* Tommy loves drawing and can't wait to attend art lessons in school. Putnam, 1997 (32p).

Diakite, Penda. *I Lost My Tooth in Africa.* This story recounts a child's trip to Mali, where she loses her tooth. Scholastic, 2006 (32p).

Figley, Marty Rhodes. *The Schoolchildren's Blizzard.* During the blizzard of 1888, a brave teacher leads her students to safety in this story based on a true event. Carolrhoda Books, 2004 (48p).

Guest, Elissa Haden. *Iris and Walter and the Field Trip.* In this early chapter book, Iris and Walter take a field trip to the aquarium. Harcourt, 2007 (48p).

Harrison, David L. *Johnny Appleseed: My Story.* In this fictionalized biography, Johnny Appleseed tells his own story to the children of a pioneer family. Random House, 2001 (48p).

Himmelman, John. *Pipaluk and the Whales.* In a story based on an actual event, a girl named Pipaluk and the people of her Arctic village help rescue beluga whales trapped in the ice. National Geographic, 2002 (32p).

Hoff, Syd. *The Littlest Leaguer.* Harold is not the biggest player on his team, but he doesn't let his size hold him back when his chance comes to show what he can do on the baseball field. HarperTrophy, 2008 (48p).

Holub, Joan. *The Pizza That We Made.* Rhyming text tells the story of three friends working together to make a pizza. Puffin, 2001 (32p).

Literature Discussion

Hulme, Joy N. *Mary Clare Likes to Share: A Math Reader.* Mary Clare uses math to share with her friends and family. Random House, 2006 (32p).

Hutchins, Pat. *The Doorbell Rang.* Sam and Victoria have to figure out how to divide a dozen cookies equally to share them with their friends. **Available in Spanish as** *Llaman a la puerta.* Harper, 1989 (32p).

Jones, Christianne C. *Room to Share.* Readers find out what happens when neat Anne and messy Gina share a room. Picture Window, 2005 (24p).

Keats, Ezra Jack. *Peter's Chair.* When Peter sees that his baby furniture is being painted pink for his new baby sister, he rescues his chair, only to discover that he has outgrown it. **Available in Spanish as** *La silla de Pedro.* Viking,1998 (40p).

Klein, Andria F. *Max Goes to the Farm.* Max and his friend Don visit Max's grandparents' farm. Picture Window, 2008 (24p).

Lin, Grace. *Lissy's Friends.* When Lissy feels lonely at school she makes an origami bird and soon has more friends than she can count. Viking, 2007 (40p).

McKissack, Robert. *Try Your Best.* On Sports Day, Ann learns the importance of trying her best. Harcourt, 2004 (24p).

McNamara, Margaret. *Dad Goes to School.* During Parents Week, the students in Ms. Connor's classroom find out what one another's parents do for a living. Aladdin, 2007 (32p).

McNamara, Margaret. *Fall Leaf Project.* The students in Mrs. Connor's class collect colorful fall leaves and send them to a class in the Southwest where leaves don't change color in the fall. Aladdin, 2006 (32p).

McNamara, Margaret. *Happy Graduation!* The first-graders at Robin Hill School celebrate their graduation with an unexpected guest. Aladdin, 2006 (32p).

Millman, Isaac. *Moses Sees a Play.* A group of hearing children visit Moses' school to see a play performed by the Little Theater of the Deaf. Insets demonstrating American Sign Language are included. Farrar, 2004 (32p).

Mora, Pat. *A Birthday Basket for Tía.* Cecilia prepares a special birthday gift for her great aunt. **Available in Spanish as** *Una canasta de cumpleaños para Tía.* Aladdin, 1997 (32p).

Nevius, Carol. *Baseball Hour.* Boys and girls find out how teamwork makes them better baseball players. Marshall Cavendish, 2008 (32p).

Osofsky, Audrey. *My Buddy.* This heartwarming picture book describes the friendship between a young boy with muscular dystrophy and his service dog. Henry Holt, 1994 (32p).

Recorvits, Helen. *My Name Is Yoon.* A Korean child adjusts to life in her new American classroom in this heartwarming narrative. Farrar, 2003 (32p).

Ries, Lori. *Aggie and Ben: Three Stories.* Ben brings home a puppy after his father surprises him with a trip to the pet store in this early chapter book. Charlesbridge, 2006 (48p).

Robbins, Jacqui. *The New Girl . . . and Me.* A friendship is born when Shakeeta joins Mia's class. Atheneum, 2006 (32p).

Rylant, Cynthia. *Mr. Putter and Tabby Run the Race.* Mr. Putter signs up for a marathon in the hopes of winning a train set. Harcourt, 2008 (44p).

Sullivan, Paula. *Todd's Box.* Todd makes a special gift for his mother. Green Light, 2004 (24p).

Tompert, Ann. *Harry's Hats.* Each time Harry puts on a new hat, he finds a new way of expressing himself. Children's Press, 2004 (32p).

Torres, Leyla. *The Kite Festival.* All of the members of Fernando's family work together to create a kite for the festival. Farrar, Straus and Giroux, 2004 (32p).

Uegaki, Chieri. *Suki's Kimono.* Suki wears a kimono to the first day of school and bravely demonstrates a traditional Japanese dance in front of her class. Kids Can, 2005 (32p).

Yaccarino, Dan. *Every Friday.* Follow a father and son on their weekly ritual of spending the day together in their urban neighborhood. Henry Holt, 2007 (32p).

Yee, Wong Herbert. *Who Likes Rain?* A girl muses about an early spring rain and the animals and things that are affected by it. Holt, 2007 (32p).

Professional Bibliography

Barrentine, Shelley. "Engaging with reading through interactive read-alouds." *The Reading Teacher, 50(1):* 36–43.

Clay, Marie M. *Becoming Literate: The Construction of Inner Control.* Heinemann, 1991.

Clay, Marie M. *Change Over Time in Children's Literacy Development.* Heinemann, 2001.

Fountas, Irene. C. and G. S. Pinnell. *Guided Reading: Good First Teaching for All Children.* Heinemann, 1996.

Fountas, Irene C. and G. S. Pinnell. *Guiding Readers and Writers: Teaching Comprehension, Genre, and Content Literacy.* Heinemann, 2001.

Fountas, Irene C. and G. S. Pinnell. *Leveled Books, K–8: Matching Texts to Readers for Effective Teaching.* Heinemann, 2005.

Fountas, Irene C. and G. S. Pinnell. *Teaching for Comprehending and Fluency: Thinking, Talking, and Writing About Reading, K–8.* Heinemann, 2006.

Holdaway, Don. *The Foundations of Literacy.* Ashton Scholastic, 1979 (also Heinemann).

Pinnell, Gay Su and Irene C. Fountas. *The Continuum of Literacy Learning, Grades K–8: Behaviors and Understandings to Notice, Teach, and Support.* Heinemann, 2007.

Teacher's Notes